Ten First Ladies
of the World

Ten First Ladies
of the World

by

PAULINE FREDERICK

Meredith Press   New York

First edition

CT
3235
.F7
1967

M MEREDITH PRESS

Library of Congress Catalog Card Number: 67-14745

MANUFACTURED IN THE UNITED STATES OF AMERICA
FOR MEREDITH PRESS

VAN REES PRESS • NEW YORK

Acknowledgments

THE AUTHOR wishes to express her gratitude to the following writers and publishers for permission to quote from their works:

Quotations in connection with Mrs. Gandhi reprinted from *Shadows on the Wall* by Krishna Nehru, copyright 1948 by The John Day Company, Inc., by permission of The John Day Company, Inc., publisher; *Toward Freedom* by Jawaharlal Nehru, copyright 1941 by The John Day Company, Inc., by permission of The John Day Company, Inc., publisher; *Glimpses of World History* by Jawaharlal Nehru, copyright 1942 by The John Day Company, Inc., by permission of The John Day Company, Inc., publisher; *A Bunch of Old Letters—Written Mostly to Jawaharlal Nehru and Some Written by Him*, copyright 1958 by Indira Gandhi, by permission of Asia Publishing House, Bombay, India, publishers; "How Mrs. Gandhi Shattered the Feminine Mystique" by Betty Friedan, *Ladies' Home*

v

Journal, May 1966, copyright © 1966 by Betty Friedan, by permission of Miss Friedan.

Quotations in connection with Mrs. Johnson reprinted from "Mrs. LBJ: A Flying Interview" by Josephine Ripley, *The Christian Science Monitor,* September 16, 1965, by permission of *The Christian Science Monitor; A Family Album* by Rebekah Baines Johnson, copyright © 1965 by Johnson City Foundation, McGraw-Hill, by permission of McGraw-Hill Book Company; "How Lady Bird Watches LBJ's Health" by Douglas Kiker, *Good Housekeeping,* May 1965, by permission of *Good Housekeeping;* "Lady Bird Writes Her Own Picture Story" by Mrs. Lyndon Baines Johnson, *Life,* Vol. 59, No. 7, August 13, 1965, copyright © 1965 by Time Inc., by permission of Time Inc.; *Mrs. LBJ* by Ruth Montgomery, Holt, Rinehart and Winston, Inc., 1964, by permission of the publishers; "My Life in the White House" by Lynda Bird Johnson, *Look,* May 18, 1965, copyright © 1965 by Lynda Bird Johnson, by permission of Miss Johnson.

Specified quotations in connection with Mrs. Wilson reprinted from articles by Kenneth Harris in *The Observer,* January 17 and February 7, 1965, by permission of The Observer Foreign News Service, London.

Quotation in connection with Mme. de Gaulle reprinted from *The De Gaulle Nobody Knows* by Alden Hatch, copyright © 1960 by Hawthorn Books, Inc., by permission of the publishers, Hawthorn Books, Inc., 70 Fifth Avenue, New York, New York.

Quotations in connection with Mme. Tito reprinted from "Tito and the Russians" by George Varjas, *Look,* July 12, 1955, by permission of Look magazine and George Varjas; *My Native Land* by Louis Adamic, Harper & Brothers, 1943, by permission of Harper & Row, Publishers, Incorporated; "The Dictator" by Helen Worden Erskine, *Collier's*, October 2, 1953, copyright 1953 by Helen Worden Erskine, by permission of Mrs. Erskine.

Quotations in connection with Mme. Nasser reprinted from *The Boss* by Robert St. John, McGraw-Hill, 1960, by permission of McGraw-Hill Book Company; *The Philosophy of the Revolution* by Gamal Abdel Nasser, Economica Books, Smith, Keynes & Marshall, 1959, by permission of Smith, Keynes & Marshall, Book Publishers.

Quotations in connection with Mme. Nkrumah reprinted from *Ghana: The Autobiography of Kwame Nkrumah*, Thomas Nelson & Sons, 1957, by permission of Thomas Nelson and Sons Limited, London.

Quotations from letters and diary of U Thant by permission of U Thant; from *Burmese Family* by Mi Mi Khaing, Indiana University Press, 1962, by permission of Indiana University Press.

Quotations in connection with Mme. Marcos reprinted from *For Every Tear a Victory: The Story of Ferdinand E. Marcos* by Hartzell Spence, McGraw-Hill, 1964, by permission of McGraw-Hill Book Company.

Contents

Introduction

A WASHINGTON CORRESPONDENT reporting the inauguration of President Rutherford B. Hayes in 1877 referred to Mrs. Hayes as the "First Lady." This is believed to be the initial application of this honorific to the wife of the man heading the Government of the United States. Hitherto the term had been used in polite society to indicate the spouse of any man. The present designation of the mistress of the White House attained popular acceptance when Charles Nirdlinger wrote in 1911 a play about Dolley Madison which he called *First Lady of the Land*.

In this American tradition the subjects have been chosen for this book. With the exception of Indira Gandhi who, as Prime Minister of India, is uniquely a first lady in her own right, the women portrayed are wives of men who exercise national power, exert regional political influence, and, in some cases, are world-shakers.

Although by American definition there are more than one

hundred first ladies in the world, only a select few have been singled out for particular attention in this collection. There are a number of reasons. It is hoped to illuminate through their wives characteristics of influential leaders that have escaped notice in the usual biographies of these men. There has been due regard for power distribution and geographical representation—to use timeworn United Nations parlance. There has been consideration for the different methods by which rulers have attained the political heights shared by their women—the coup, the revolution, and the democratic process. There has been particular interest in the unusual attributes of the first ladies themselves—the former beauty queen, the one-time guerrilla fighter, the devout Buddhist. There are included, also, skillful politicians and those who by tradition, choice, or direction of their husbands remain in the secluded shadows, avoiding public exposure as much as possible.

Some of the first ladies presented herein have shared the pinnacle of power with their husbands for a long time. Others have entered upon the world stage knowing that their husbands' tenures were limited by law or constitution.

Madame Nkrumah's sojourn in Accra was suddenly terminated by the unpredictability of African politics. Overnight her all-powerful husband became a man without a country; she was suddenly an expatriate who found it necessary to return to her native Egypt, which, one suspects, she was not reluctant to do. She is no longer a first lady, but her story is included because of the strange, occult influence that brought her—a stranger—to Ghana.

To the first ladies and those persons who know them and were willing to cooperate in this undertaking, I wish to express my gratitude. To the first ladies of countries where officials were too frightened to provide even noncontroversial curricula vitae—one, because another first lady was to appear in the book—I offer appreciation for the challenge to try to uncover facts that have not been available to the general public.

In assuming this task, which, at times, seemed to present insurmountable obstacles in obtaining source material, I must acknowledge that my greatest help came from one who is a first lady in research and suggestions. Thank you most of all, Leonore Silvian.

P. F.

Ten First Ladies
of the World

1.

Indira Gandhi—India

W<small>HEN</small> Indira Nehru Gandhi was born on November 19, 1917, astrologers said she was marked for leadership. A unique combination of heritage and a backwash from World War I that swept India shortly after her birth was to bring fulfillment of the prophecy.

Indira made her debut into a Kashmiri family of wealth and the highest Hindu caste on the estate of her grandfather in Allahabad where the sacred Ganges meets the Jumna. Pandit Motilal Nehru had acquired an international reputation and fortune by his brilliance at the bar, commanding deference from the judges at the High Court sitting in the ancient city and intellectuals at home and abroad. He was to help shape a historic career for his granddaughter.

Motilal Nehru enjoyed a life like that of a wealthy British aristocrat in his elegantly furnished Anand Bhawan (House of Happiness) with its wide verandas, spacious gardens, tennis courts, swimming pools, and stables filled with horses, car-

Indira Gandhi

riages, and cars. His love of pomp had been displayed at the elaborate wedding in 1916 for his dearly loved only son, Jawaharlal. Indira's grandfather had spotted her mother at a special breakfast for prospective brides of Kashmiri Brahmins in Delhi. Kamala Kaul, daughter of a businessman, was pretty. However, her background was Orthodox, lacking the Western influence, social and educational experience of the Nehru heir. The governesses of the Nehru daughters—Swarup and Krishna— were enlisted to try to remedy these deficiencies.

Indira was to hear about the great bustle over the wedding which was set for the auspicious date of February 8, *Vasanta Panchami*, herald of spring and sponsor of music and the arts. Months before the event, jewelers, tailors, and merchants brought their wares to the house, and clerks arrived to supplement the retinue of servants in preparing for the elaborate occasion. One week before the ceremony, her grandfather hired a special train to take more than a hundred guests to Delhi, where hundreds more were waiting. Tents were set up to provide accommodations, and this was called the Nehru Wedding Camp. There were ten days of festivities, and then the train returned to Allahabad with its celebrants for still more parties. Her parents went to Kashmir for the honeymoon. They were soon joined by her grandfather and a host of friends whom he took aboard a fleet of houseboats.

Finally, Kamala and Jawaharlal returned to Anand Bhawan to set up housekeeping. Indira was born there. She was soon to realize that her legacy was not only wealth and position. The house was a political center where her grandfather and father and their friends discussed the future of an India free of colonial rule.

Motilal was president of the local Home Rule League and Jawaharlal was its secretary. They wanted at least as much freedom for India as British dominions enjoyed. The British government had found it expedient to offer a promissory note of dominion status to ensure Indian cooperation in the war in Europe. When that conflict was over, however, the debtor was in no hurry to pay up. It was then that the tiny child Indira would be awakened by angry talk between her father and grandfather about what should be done. Both were noted for their tempers and vigorous, differing opinions on how to achieve independence.

Indira's grandfather deeply loved her father—she was to learn that Mahatma Gandhi called this love divine—but this did not prevent the two men from arguing heatedly about how to compel Britain to fulfill its commitment. Motilal, the lawyer, favored working for change by legal means. Jawaharlal was sure that defiance of the authorities preached by Gandhi was the most effective course. Motilal could not bear the thought of his son going to jail for breaking the law. It became obvious that the grandfather's position at this time was motivated as much by concern for his son's welfare as political gain for India when he sometimes slept on the floor to see what prison life would be like for Jawaharlal.

Indira was scarcely two when her grandfather invited Gandhi to Anand Bhawan to talk with him alone about the pros and cons of the civil disobedience campaign and the hazards her father faced if he should participate. Afterward, Gandhi advised Jawaharlal not to press his views to a breaking point with Motilal. As it soon turned out, this was not necessary. Indira was three when police brutality against Indian demonstrators brought her grandfather to a momentous decision. He announced he would cast his lot, also, with Gandhi.

When Indira was four, she had the first of what were to be many experiences with the police as a result of her family's course. On the night of December 6, 1921, officers of the law entered and searched Anand Bhawan and took her father and grandfather to jail for distributing literature calling for non-cooperation and for belonging to the now subversive Home Rule League. The next day she sat in her grandfather's lap before the District Magistrate and heard a shamefaced former Indian colleague of the renowned Motilal ask that he be punished for breaking the law. Her father and grandfather were sentenced to six months in prison.

Jawaharlal was concerned about the effect of such incidents on his little girl, whom he had lovingly nicknamed Indu, meaning "Moon." He wrote down his thoughts, "Soon after our arrest in December 1921 the police started paying frequent visits to Anand Bhawan. They came to realize the fines which had been imposed on Father and me. It was the Congress' policy not to pay fines. So the police came day after day and attached and carried away bits of furniture. Indira, my four-year-old daughter, was greatly annoyed at this continuous procession of despoliation and protested to the police, and expressed her strong displeasure. I am afraid those early impressions are likely to color her future views about the police force generally."

Indira had inherited the Nehru temper and imperious manner, both of which she readily displayed toward the British intruders. And she had many opportunities. Her father served nine prison sentences between 1921 and 1945—from the time his daughter was four until she was twenty-eight. The grandfather, whom Indira loved for what she was to describe as "his bigness . . . he seemed to embrace the whole world," and for the way he laughed, was in and out of jail until he died in 1931. And her frail mother, who picketed in the heat and dust of Allahabad when she had tuberculosis, also knew prison life.

When a caller at Anand Bhawan asked why the house was so deserted, Indira retorted, "What else could it be when Papa, Mama and Grandpa are all in prison?"

Life at Anand Bhawan became very different when Indira's grandfather led the family into the Gandhi camp. Her Aunt Krishna described it this way: "Father ... gave up his large practise at the bar. This changed our life, which until then had been of ease and luxury, to one of simplicity and a little hardship. Father had earned millions and had also spent lavishly, never hoarding up money for a rainy day. When he gave up his practise, we immediately had to bring about certain changes in the household as it was not possible to live as we had been doing, with no income at all. The first thing Father did was to sell his horses and carriages ... then we had to dismiss quite a few of the army of servants we had to curtail expenses. ... There were no more banquets; only one cook instead of two or three, and no more smart butlers with numerous bearers ... all our lovely Dresden and Venetian china and glass and many other articles both expensive and beautiful were sold off and we had to get used to fewer servants and less of the luxuries of daily life ... quite a few of our wealthy friends kept away, and where one saw riches and wealth before, one now saw khadi-clad men and women, simple and humble."

Moreover, as an act of defiance, carloads of Western finery were consigned to bonfires as the women of the Nehru family donned the humble, rough homespun which was a mark of their new political affiliation. Indira was faced with a painful choice when her mother told her she must decide whether to keep a dress brought from Paris by Aunt Swarup, who was now Mme. Ranjit Pandit, or sacrifice it, too. It was not without inner turmoil that the youngster placed politics above vanity.

Under the circumstances, Indira's childhood was a lonely one.

She was separated from her loved ones and at the same time isolated, because of her youth, from the cause that had taken them from her. She tried to compensate for this at first by making haughty speeches about Indian independence to any servants within hearing and playing a game of civil disobedience and arrest with her dolls. When she was twelve she tried to join the Congress Party but was turned down. In a burst of anger she organized the Monkey Brigade. The idea was suggested by the legend about monkeys which built a bridge from India to Ceylon to help the Rama rescue his wife from abduction by the King of Ceylon. The youngsters took on the job of trying to help the cause of the grown-ups by writing notices, addressing envelopes, making flags, carrying water and messages, and serving as spies. As the latter, they infiltrated "the enemy," pretending to play hopscotch while listening for some careless word about a planned arrest or raid. When they overheard pertinent intelligence, they quietly stole out of sight and then ran to alert the persons concerned.

Indira's education was erratic. It started with kindergarten in Delhi, and there was also a brief period at a convent school. From 1923 to 1930 her father was out of jail, but Indira's life was far from normal, since Jawaharlal was away from home most of the time because of his political activity all over India. A baby brother was born in 1924, who lived only a few days. Then it was discovered that Indira's mother had tuberculosis. The family decided to take her to Switzerland to enter a sanitarium, and Indira went to school there. On their return nearly two years later a new Anand Bhawan was being built for them by Grandfather Motilal across the road from the original house which he had given to the nation. In 1929 Indira's father succeeded her grandfather as President of the Congress Party and one year later was back in jail.

It was during the period from October 1930 to August 1933, when Jawaharlal served terms in four different prisons that he decided to occupy his time by writing letters about world history to his daughter, whose education he had not been able to supervise. He explained to Indira at the outset that this undertaking was "not meant to teach you history, but just to give you glimpses of it and to awaken your curiosity." Indira saw most of the 196 letters only after her father's release in 1933, since jail mail service was virtually nonexistent.

The first letter was written on Indira's thirteenth birthday by Samvat reckoning—October 26, 1930. It regretted that the father's gifts could not be material. He said that instead they were "of the air and of the mind and spirit, such as a good fairy might have bestowed." He spoke of her good fortune in being "a witness to this great struggle for freedom" and "in having a very brave and wonderful little woman for your Mummie." It closed, "Goodbye, little one, and may you grow up into a brave soldier in India's service."

On New Year's Day 1931 Jawaharlal wrote Indira that he had received the news that "Mummie" had been arrested and taken to jail. He said, "It was a pleasant New Year's gift for me. It had long been expected and I have no doubt that Mummie is thoroughly happy and contented.

"But you must be rather lonely. Once a fortnight you may see Mummie and once a fortnight you may see me, and you will carry our messages to each other."

Indira had been sent to boarding school in Poona with Mme. Pandit's daughters when it became apparent that her mother and aunts were to go to prison. She had begged the police unsuccessfully to arrest her, too, so that she could be "included."

This separation was not to be a long one, for Indira's parents were released in a general amnesty. They probably would have been allowed to go home anyway because the great Motilal was dying. When this pillar of the House of Nehru fell, the grieving child and her father and mother sailed for Ceylon. When they returned her father once more went to jail.

Indira then attended a school conducted by the revered poet, Sir Rabindranath Tagore. However, her mother's health began to fail seriously in 1935 and they decided to return to Switzerland, which required Indira to transfer to a school there. Tagore wrote her father: "It is with a heavy heart we bade farewell to Indira, for she was such an asset in our place. I have watched her very closely and have felt admiration for the way you have brought her up. Her teachers, all in one voice, praise her and I know she is extremely popular with the students. I only hope things will turn for the better and she will soon return here and get back to her studies."

Indira and her father were with Kamala when she died in Lausanne on February 28, 1936. Father and daughter were drawn even closer together by the bereavement. They went to Montreux for a few days and then to England, where Indira entered school. She was to finish her education—in history—at Oxford, where she also took part in the student movement. At twenty-one, she achieved an early political ambition. She became a member of the Congress Party. She also disclosed a deep humanitarian concern which has characterized much of her public activity since. She established child care and welfare centers.

By her own account, Indira Nehru did not think seriously of marriage until she was eighteen or nineteen—"not because my father was away, but because I felt I should devote every minute to the political struggle, and marriage would come in the way." But in 1942 Feroze Gandhi—who was not related to the Mahatma—persuaded her otherwise. He was a journalist and lawyer born in Bombay who had worked with her mother for independence in Allahabad. He was also a Parsi, a believer in the teachings of Zoroaster. Many Orthodox Indians considered this an inferior religion, although the secular-minded Nehrus had already accepted a Parsi in the family, Raja Hutheesing, the husband of Indira's Aunt Krishna. However, the prominence of Jawaharlal attracted attention to Indira's choice and stirred nationwide controversy. She relates that although her "father never said anything one way or the other, in the beginning he was not very happy. But others were very much against it. And the whole country was against it."

Gandhi, the holy man to many Indians, who was very close to both Indira and her father, received many letters about the impending marriage, admitting "some are dreadful." Nehru sought Gandhi's advice about having a small, quiet wedding as Indira wished. The Mahatma suggested that since the match was so controversial, people would think Jawaharlal did not want to do anything for his daughter and son-in-law if the occasion were not made important. Although the wedding was not "in the grand manner" of Jawaharlal's, it was a large one to which people from all over India were invited.

The Gandhis went to Kashmir for their honeymoon. And then, ironically enough, Indira was to have the wish fulfilled that she had held since she was a little girl. She was sent to prison—as was her husband—for taking part in the "Quit India" movement directed at the British. Their marriage began in separate jails.

Indira confesses that imprisonment offered a completeness she had been seeking. Long before, she had made up her mind that she had to go to prison. It was a mark of national honor. Now she was shut in with hardened criminals—even murderers. At last she was "included." Behind the gray walls, Indira soon displayed the Nehru bent for leadership. She forbade the twenty-two other chattering women to speak to her before five o'clock in the afternoon. She began to teach them to read and write, and even instructed a few in politics. She tried out her newly acquired knowledge of baby care on the month-and-a-half-old infant of a young mother. She wanted to adopt the child, but her relatives felt this would be too much of a burden.

After thirteen months in prison, Indira and her husband were released and went to Allahabad to live. Two sons were born—Rajiv in 1944 and Sanjay in 1946. Like their parents, they were educated at Cambridge. In 1947, Indira moved into her father's house in Delhi as his hostess. Feroze stayed with them for a time but decided to set up his own establishment when he entered parliament. There was never a divorce. He died in 1960.

Indira recently talked about her marriage to an American woman.*

> It wasn't an ideally happy marriage. We were very happy at times. We quarreled tremendously at times. It was partly because both of us were so headstrong, and partly circumstances. I wouldn't have gone into public life if he had said no. But I am so intense in whatever I do, he must have been frightened to have it all concentrated on him. He wanted me occupied. He was very occupied with his own career. But when I went into public life, and became successful, he liked it and he didn't like it. Other people—friends, relatives—were the worst. They would say, "How does it feel, being so-and-so's husband?" He would get upset, and it would take me weeks to win him over. To hurt the male ego is, of course, the biggest sin in marriage.
>
> He was not a person who discusses these things. He was a very good political speaker on any issue, but this

* Betty Friedan, *Ladies' Home Journal*, May 1966.

kind of thing, about feelings and so on, he could not speak. But, toward the end, we were somehow getting beyond all this and becoming very close. The summer before he died, we had a nearly perfect holiday.

As August 14, 1947, passed into August 15 at midnight, Indira Gandhi witnessed a great moment in Indian history. Her father made his first speech to the new free Parliament of the Dominion of India. He was the first Prime Minister. The slim, small figure with the sharp features and dark melancholy eyes who listened said afterward she was so excited and proud she thought she would burst. When asked if this was because she was an Indian or the daughter of Jawaharlal Nehru, she replied, "I think it was really all mixed up. I can't really separate the two personalities. But more as an Indian, I think, because of having taken part in the struggle and to feel it was worth it."

As hostess for the Prime Minister Indira became the chatelaine of the large demanding household of the official residence, once the home of the British commander in chief. The main floor was occupied by reception rooms, offices, and studies, with the living quarters overhead. She decorated the mansion for her father's comfort and enjoyment, introducing reminders of his career, like the doll collection in regional Indian costumes, the Bengal pottery horse, and curtains woven by the peasants. There were pictures by modern Indian artists, a photograph of Lord Louis and Lady Mountbatten, his closest friends, and a sketch of Kamala. She had a daughter's concern for the well-being of her father. She once said, "I do not like my father to be careless about his health. I have to get angry at him very often. I sometimes have to drag him out of his office at midnight." She was at her father's side to receive official guests in Delhi and traveled abroad with him twenty-four times on visits to foreign capitals from Washington to Peking.

Indira Gandhi once said she looked on politics as "something which could not be avoided." This was even more true when she moved into her father's house in Delhi than it had been when she was growing up at Anand Bhawan. She had become the confidante of India's Prime Minister and was at the vortex of all the issues swirling about the world's largest democracy. She could, and did, influence policy. Her unique position is believed by some people to account for her failure to make close friends. She was too suspicious that others might seek to cultivate her merely to gain access to her father. She is reported to have contested rivals like Krishna Menon for her father's favor. Her relations were not always cordial with her politically oriented aunt, Mrs. Pandit, who was India's first woman Minister and Ambassador, and the only one of her sex to be elected President of the United Nations General Assembly. To those who could break through her reserve Indira was warm and friendly, but she could be arrogant and imperious. One who understands her explains, "Indira does not suffer fools gladly and it shows."

Mrs. Gandhi's political activity was not confined to councils of state where decisions were made. She had her father's courage to walk fearlessly among the people to try to discover the causes of trouble as a step toward formulating remedies. After the Hindu-Muslim riots in Delhi following partition she worked under Gandhi to arrange a meeting between the warring factions. She took students to the Indian-Tibetan border in 1956 to introduce a welfare program among the primitive tribesmen. She was at the front in the Chinese-Indian war to direct civilian assistance and encourage the troops. She was on the scene where there were food riots, separatist uprisings, and violence over language regulations. She had acquired her father's ability to establish a kind of mystical communion with the masses, moving with firmness among them, drawing inspiration and strength from the contact which sharpened her communication with the people.

In 1959 Indira received full redress from the Congress Party for refusing her membership when she was twelve. Unanimously, she was elected Congress President and thus followed in the footsteps of her father and grandfather. Prime Minister Nehru did not oppose her election, although he said afterward that he thought it was not a fortunate precedent for India. However, he conceded that it represented an effort to make use of the abilities of the younger generation in the party leadership. There were some charges of nepotism. Indira showed in the year of her service that she was not only the daughter of her father but a person of political ability in her own right. She tightened up the sprawling bureaucracy and gave the organization a firmer program for the country. She left the post on ground of ill health, but people who said she was frail were aware of her retort, "Those who have watched me grow up know I can be frail and hardy at the same time."

On May 27, 1964, Jawaharlal Nehru died, and his daughter experienced a sensation of numbness for months. It is reported that she was offered her father's post three times but turned it down. She said, "I am not modest enough to say that I cannot handle the job, but I am not conceited enough to say that others cannot handle it." Prime Minister Shastri finally prevailed on her to become Minister of Broadcasting and Information, after she had declined his first offer of the Foreign Ministry portfolio. She assented because she did not wish to give the impression she was not ready to cooperate with the new government.

Then on January 11, 1966, Shastri died in Tashkent after signing an agreement with Pakistan to try to bring the dispute over Kashmir to an end. The politicians assembled in the circular hall of Parliament in New Delhi to choose a new leader.

The slight woman with the brooding eyes who had listened to her father so many times in this chamber since that memorable midnight in 1947, sat toward the rear. There was now a streak of gray in her dark hair, and a Nehru red rose was pinned to the brown Kashmiri shawl gathered over her white sari. She watched 526 of her colleagues walk to the dais in twos and threes to put their ballots in a wooden box. She thought of the poem by Robert Frost:

> The King said to his son: "Enough of this!
> The Kingdom's yours to finish as you please.
> I'm getting out tonight. Here, take the crown."
> But the Prince drew away his hand in time
> To avoid what he wasn't sure he wanted.

Two and a half hours later the crown was hers nonetheless. Some said it was a crown of thorns. She arose and said quietly, "My heart is full and I do not know how to thank you. . . . As I stand before you, my thoughts go to the great leaders—Mahatma Gandhi at whose feet I grew up; Panditji, my father, and Lal Bahadur Shastri. . . . These leaders have shown us the way and I want to go along the same path."

Someone asked what it was like to be the first woman Prime Minister of India. She responded sharply, "It is a question of being a human being, not a man or woman."

Lady Bird Johnson

2.

Lady Bird Johnson–
United States

A WORRIED American mother wrote of her anxiety about the Vietnam war to the wife of the President of the United States. She received a noncommital reply from the White House signed by foreign affairs spokesman McGeorge Bundy. The rerouting of such correspondence is an indication of the care Mrs. Lyndon Baines Johnson exercises in avoiding controversy though she has been called the most active and politically minded mistress of the White House since Eleanor Roosevelt. Lady Bird's caution is dictated primarily by concern for the political welfare of the huge Texan she married more than thirty years ago. She studiously shies away from involvement in causes about which there are sharp divisions of opinion so as not to add to any criticism of her husband. Consequently, her activities outside the big house at 1600 Pennsylvania Avenue in Washington are confined to comparatively "safe" projects

19

like Head Start, poverty, highway beautification, and conservation. Any references to potentially contentious matters like civil rights and peace are kept on a highly idealistic plateau. Even if her loyalty to the "boss" were not so intense, she long ago learned what LBJ's official family has since found out: there is only one authority on important issues while Lyndon B. Johnson is President. Much as he esteems Franklin D. Roosevelt as the father figure to be emulated, this does not include following FDR's example of accepting philosophically a wife's propensity to express herself freely on all questions.

Mrs. Johnson early laid down for herself and her daughters a rule of public prudence to which she adheres strictly. Younger daughter Luci remembers as a little girl her mother's constant counsel, "Never say anything you don't want quoted on page one of the newspaper." This was long before she dreamed that any of their remarks might ever be considered news.

Mrs. Johnson is also modest about the extent of her own knowledge, once citing this as a reason for her reluctance to discuss with her husband such complicated problems as Vietnam. She told an interviewer, ". . . I know I cannot solve them. I know enough to try to give solace to Lyndon who has to work at solving them, so I can listen to him intelligently." * She has confessed candidly that the President does not seek her advice on these matters, he just talks to her "in the manner of a man weighing the pros and cons. He just talks them out. It is not that I can advise." * A First Family watcher has remarked, ". . . It is fairly plain that the President does not ask the First Lady about the advisability of sending ground troops to Vietnam."

In view of this accepted limitation on conversation, Mrs. Johnson's tea for Mme. Chiang Kai-shek at the White House in September 1965 must have been a little bitter for the Chinese

* Josephine Ripley, "Mrs. LBJ; A Flying Interview," *The Christian Science Monitor*, September 16, 1965.

dowager if she sought reassurance for the cause and status of the Chinese nationalists. The visit preceded the UN Assembly's largest vote in favor of seating the Communists, and polls were beginning to show American opinion leaning toward recognition of the government in Peking. The official White House report of the teacup agenda disclosed only the following topics: the beauty of the autumn, the First Lady's recent trip to the Grand Tetons, the visit of Vice President and Mrs. Johnson to Taiwan in 1961, their enjoyment of a pedicab ride, and the delicious frogs' legs grown in the canals running between the rice paddies.

While Mrs. Johnson eschews the substance of diplomacy, she demonstrates a native tact that is an asset in the profession. This came to the fore on an April day in 1963, when United Nations delegates from twenty-five countries were the guests of the then Vice President and his wife at their Texas ranch. Visitors to the Johnson home always go on a tour of the LBJ acres on the Pedernales. This particular safari started with the Vice President leading eight of the party on horseback while Mrs. Johnson shepherded the rest into a school bus that had been borrowed from Johnson City. When the two groups suddenly converged, the horse carrying Torbjorn Christiansen, First Secretary of the Norwegian delegation, reared and threw its rider. After Lady Bird had made sure that the diplomat was not injured, she recalled an incident to ease his embarrassment. "That reminds me of the time Lyndon was asked to ride at the head of a parade in Austin," she said. "As he rode by, a rancher sitting on the curb said, 'Look at old Lyndon, you can sure tell he's rode a lot.' Just then the horse shied, and Lyndon had difficulty controlling him. Observing this, another rancher interjected, 'Yes, but not lately.' "

At the typical Johnson barbecue following the tour, the Ambassador from Ceylon, G. P. Malalasekera, responded to a toast from the host. His words indicated the impression Mrs. Johnson had made on the guests. Malalasekera said, ". . . We have a saying—'a man's wife is his strength, his inspiration, and his good angel.' Mr. Vice President, I think you have been extremely lucky. . . ." Lyndon Johnson must agree. He vows, "She is still the most enjoyable woman I have ever known. As a sweetheart, swimmer, boat rider, and conversationalist, she is the most interesting woman I know." He grants his wife a privilege which no one else can exercise with impunity—the right to criticize him. But he somewhat overstates the case when he says, "She is the first to tell me about any mistakes, whether they are financial extravagances or a political boner, and to me that is the test of real character." Lady Bird employs this authority with discretion. She finds that it is wisest to confine her chiding of an overly sensitive man largely to matters of health, with occasional reminders of the importance of good relations with the press.

During the 1960 political campaign one critic saw personal ambition dominating Lady Bird's devotion to her husband. He said, "I felt she cared more about her husband's career than her husband. She's got very darting eyes, you know. I had a feeling of somebody who was making all kinds of long mental notes, almost a human tape recorder going." However, it is difficult to separate the person and the career of the roughhewn, hard-driving man who became the thirty-sixth President of the United States. Lyndon Johnson's life is politics, as Claudia Alta Taylor learned when she married him on Nov. 17, 1934, after a courtship as swift as a Texas sandstorm.

In the summer of 1934, Lady Bird Taylor, having long before ". . . made . . . peace with the nickname" bestowed on her by a family servant, left Karnack, Texas, for Washington, D.C. She possessed a fresh bachelor's degree in journalism from the University of Texas, and the trip to the capital was a graduation gift from her father. She carried the name and phone number of a young man whom her Austin friend, Mrs. Gene Lassater, said would be "a wonderful guy to show her the town." Gene had also taken care to drop a note to the man in question, telling him to expect a call from the daughter of Thomas Jefferson Taylor. But Lady Bird never followed through. As a Texan she might have been prone to adventure, but a strain of Southern gentility from her mother's side of the family restrained her from contacting a stranger.

Lady Bird had grown up with these conflicting influences. Her father encouraged self-reliance. When she was six, he sent her alone on a long train trip to visit relatives in Alabama. He gave her a pony to ride to the one-room school which she attended from the first to the seventh grade with tenant farmers' children. She had a car at thirteen to drive to junior high school, an unlimited charge account at Neiman-Marcus while she went to finishing school in Dallas and the university in Austin. She had much the same freedom and instruction at a corresponding age as that enjoyed by her brothers, Tom, Jr., and Antonio, eight and eleven years her senior. On the other hand, maiden Aunt Effie Pattillo of the Alabama gentry, who took over much of Bird's upbringing after her mother's death, when the child was six, emphasized traditional Southern breeding for a young lady. Shy feminine charm and dependence on the male were qualities to be encouraged, in Miss Effie's view.

After returning from Washington, where she did not meet the "wonderful guy," Bird undertook an assignment from her father to redecorate Brick House, their antebellum plantation manor near Karnack in eastern Texas, not far from the Mississippi border. She went to Austin to consult an architect and was visiting in Gene Lassater's office when lanky six-foot-three Lyndon Baines Johnson walked in. He was Executive Secretary to Congressman Richard M. Kleberg of Texas—and the man Bird was supposed to have called in Washington. Introductions were made, and Johnson asked Miss Taylor and Mrs. Lassater to have coffee with him. He then suggested that Bird breakfast with him the next morning. At that time he said he was going to take her to San Marcos the following day to see his parents.

Bird recalls her first meeting with her future mother-in-law. She says, "The first time I met Lyndon's mother, I felt a sympathetic urge to lift the tension between us. I remember it so well because I could see the uncertainty in his mother's face and almost hear the unspoken questions, 'What is he bringing into my life? Is my son seriously interested in this young woman?'

"She idolized him. She had five children, and she was a very great, a very devoted mother to all of them. But I think maybe Lyndon meant more to her—she never would admit it!—than the rest of them."

LBJ had made up his mind about Miss Taylor. To press his suit he carried Bird off to meet his boss at the King Ranch—Kleberg was part owner of the fabulous holding. Then it was time to clinch his campaign by facing her father. He induced a friend to drive his car and pick him up at the plantation so he could chauffeur his girl to Karnack, where big Tom Taylor advertised himself as "a dealer in everything" in the sign across his general store. Bird's father also owned cotton gin mills and considerable land. After dinner the young man from western Texas proposed to the girl with the soft voice and gentle manner. He did not win a definite answer, but next morning before starting back to Washington he received a good-bye kiss.

Lyndon Johnson returned to the capital to pursue his courtship by telephone via the Karnack party line. Aunt Effie advised her niece not to rush into marriage. But Tom Taylor was a practical man. He told Bird, "... some of the best deals are made in a hurry." Two months after their first date, Johnson decided to act. He left Washington for Texas. En route, at 8 A.M., on Saturday morning, November 17, 1934, he telephoned Postmaster James Quill of San Antonio to say he and Lady Bird would be married in St. Mark's Church in San Antonio at six o'clock that evening. He wanted Quill to make the necessary arrangements. Lyndon then picked up Bird in Karnack. She had not yet said Yes but agreed to go with him to Austin. On the way, he persuaded her to be his bride, and they changed their destination to San Antonio. At the church they met Quill, who did not have a ring. When LBJ remonstrated with the best man, the latter retorted, "Why didn't you get it yourself? You've been passing jewelry stores all day." The wedding was saved when Quill went to Sears Roebuck and bought a ring for $2.98. A few minutes later twenty-one-year-old Claudia Alta Taylor became the wife of twenty-six-year-old Lyndon Baines Johnson.

Following a honeymoon in Mexico, the young couple set up housekeeping in a one-bedroom apartment in Washington. Lyndon's salary was $267 a month, out of which he spent $100 for lunches, night law-school tuition, payment and upkeep of the car. From what was left the bride managed to save $18.75 a month for a government bond after meeting the bills for rent, food, clothes, and entertainment of relatives and friends. At first, the ambitious young husband did not fully appreciate the skillful business manager he had married. Nevertheless, by background and experience Bird had unusual qualifications in this area. She had inherited her father's shrewd way with money and learned his successful methods. She has said, "Fall was the financial high point of our year. This was the time when we would go to the bank to pay off our loans and use the rest of the money to buy adjoining land." * Moreover, her mother's bach-

* Ruth Montgomery, *Mrs. LBJ*, Holt, Rinehart & Winston, New York, 1964.

elor brother, for whom she was named, had stimulated Bird's interest in high finance, teaching her to study stock quotations before she was twelve and encouraging her to read books on economics. Uncle Claude Pattillo had hoped his bright niece would go on to the Harvard School of Business Administration. However, she opted for Lyndon Johnson. And she did remarkably well for him with what she already knew about finances and studious application to the job. She is given substantial credit for parlaying a modest inheritance and some Alabama land into a multimillion-dollar estate with radio and television stations, ranches and a substantial stock portfolio—all of which were put under trusteeship when Lyndon Johnson became President.

Nine months after their marriage, Johnson resigned as assistant to Congressman Kleberg to return to Austin as head of the National Youth Administration in Texas. When Congressman James P. Buchanan of the Tenth District died in 1937, LBJ decided to run for the vacancy. Bird borrowed ten thousand dollars against her inheritance to make his campaign possible. She accompanied her husband on most of his dawn-to-dusk stumping, but she was too shy to campaign personally. Besides, she has said, "In 1937, it simply wasn't done in Texas. . . ."

Lady Bird learned politics quickly from a master—her husband. Her first lesson was to memorize the names, faces and positions of all the important politicians in the district. While it was still an ordeal for her to make speeches and ask for votes, she contrived a plan to attain her objectives. She would drive into a filling station and ask for a few gallons of gasoline. While the attendants replenished the tank, wiped the windshield, and checked the oil, she engaged them in friendly chatter, finally suggesting that they vote for her favorite candidate. Then she would drive on to the next station and repeat the ploy. Mrs. John Connally, wife of the future governor of Texas, went on this first gasoline canvas with Bird. Later, they shared an apartment in Washington when their husbands were in the service.

On April 10, 1937, two days after being operated on for appendicitis, Lyndon Johnson was elected to the House of Representatives. He and Lady Bird went back to the capital for an unbroken tenure that took them to the White House in 1963.

Mrs. Johnson became active in her husband's campaigning for the first time in the Senate race of 1948, when he squeaked through by eighty-seven votes (which were unsuccessfully contested). He had first been defeated for the Senate in 1941 but stayed on in the House. Senator Johnson gave his wife credit for his victory. He told how she organized women, and although she hated air travel because it made her sick, she flew all over the state. He remembered particularly that the night before election a car in which she was riding overturned twice. He said: "She got out of the mud, stood in a reception line in a dress borrowed from her hostess, and then joined me in San Antonio to make a speech. She didn't even tell me about the accident. ... When she got back to the hotel around midnight ... we said she had to go on to Austin that night to do some last-minute campaigning in the morning. As she changed for the trip I saw those big bruises, and she had to confess." The determined campaigner for Lyndon Johnson went right on to Austin and got on the telephone. She and his mother and sisters called about everyone in the Austin phone book. Her husband concedes, "We carried Austin three-to-one, thanks to that, but we barely carried the state." *

By 1960 Bird Johnson was a proved financial and political asset to her husband. She started taking speech lessons with her friend Scooter Miller of Texas, to increase her platform confi-

* *Ibid.*

dence. She went on a full campaign schedule to try to help LBJ win the Democratic Presidential nomination. At a Democratic Women's dinner in May of that year she said:

> This is a brand-new experience for me. Usually at a dinner like this, I listen to someone introduce Lyndon with words of praise and approval, all of which I underwrite and enjoy. But I want to introduce him in a more personal way—as an exciting man to live with; an exhausting man to keep up with; a man who has worn well in the twenty-five years we've been together; and, most important, a man from whom I've learned that to put all the brains and heart and skill you have into the job of trying to make your government work a little better can be a wonderful life for a man, and his wife. My friends, may I introduce my husband, Lyndon B. Johnson.

When Lyndon Johnson was relegated to second place on the presidential ticket, his wife loyally campaigned for the party. Robert Kennedy said, "Lady Bird carried Texas for us."

In the Presidential election year of 1964, the woman who had become the First Lady traveled 45,348 miles by herself as "an extra set of eyes and ears" for the President. She also accompanied her husband 31,000 additional miles that took them to 121 towns and cities in 35 states. She was called a "consummate politician" by one observer, while another said, "She has few peers as a spotter of trouble and a knower of whom to call."

Mrs. Johnson's political and public activities are always meant to serve her first loyalty—that to her husband. Her role as wife to Lyndon Baines Johnson is paramount. When the then Senate Majority Leader suffered a severe heart attack in 1955, she was at his side constantly. The doctors ordered their patient to lose weight, so Lady Bird joined in the dieting. When as President of the United States he was taken to Bethesda Naval Hospital by ambulance in the middle of the night with a heavy cold following a strenuous round of inauguration ceremonies, Mrs. Johnson was at Camp David. She was notified immediately by the White House physician, against the President's express orders. The next morning she arrived at the hospital and checked in as a patient with a cold also, remaining close to her husband until his discharge. When the President underwent his kidneystone and gall-bladder operation in the fall of 1965, his wife was with him in the hospital and then, tearing up her calendar for the rest of the year, went with him to the ranch to supervise his recuperation. Her constant concern for his health is a muchtold tale. One incident shows the tact and persistence which she uses in trying to take care of a man who demands as much of himself as he does of the overpressured people around him. Douglas Kiker reports that once during a particularly tiring campaign swing LBJ called the four pool reporters into the private cabin of *Air Force One* after the plane was airborne. He began to talk. "After half an hour, Mrs. Johnson quietly suggested that, since this flight leg was a fairly long one, the President might like to catch a little nap. He agreed, but kept on talking.

"A few minutes later, Mrs. Johnson went to him and, without saying a word, helped him off with his coat and loosened his necktie.... The reporters rose to leave, but the President waved them back to their seats.

"Finally, the First Lady approached him again. This time she removed his tie from around his neck and started unbuttoning his shirt. 'I think Mrs. Johnson is hinting that it's time for me to take a nap,' the President said. The reporters fled. Mr. Johnson got his rest." *

Their daughters were much-wanted children after the decade

* Douglas Kiker, *Good Housekeeping*, May 1965.

of travail Mrs. Johnson went through before they were born. Her husband once disclosed, "She waited ten years to have a baby and has lost four children with miscarriages. She is never a person who admits her own pain."

Lynda Bird was born in Garfield Hospital, Washington, on March 19, 1944. Lucy Baines arrived on July 2, 1947. The two sisters are very different—physically as well as in their personalities. Lynda, who has brown hair and brown eyes, grew to be 5 feet 9½ inches tall, while Luci—who as an independent teenager changed the spelling of her first name—has brown hair and blue eyes and is only 5 feet 3½ inches tall. Lynda showed a special interest in serious historical research, being graduated from the University of Texas in 1966, going on special archeological surveys in the West during vacation periods, and offering her parents literary and historical quotations for their speeches from time to time. Luci was more oriented toward the homemaking interests of cooking and sewing and liked to read sentimental poems of her own composition to her father and mother.

There was little in the experience of Lady Bird Johnson to prepare her fully for the sudden upheaval of her family's life on November 22, 1963. She was riding with her husband in the official cavalcade in Dallas when the assassin's bullets struck down President Kennedy in the car ahead. There was the blur of shock and disbelief as they raced toward Parkland Hospital, bent below window level on order of the Secret Service. Then came the ride to the airport under the kind of protection that is provided only for the President of the United States and his family. In less than two hours after the shots were fired, she stood inside the cabin of *Air Force One* beside her husband as he raised his right hand, placed his left on the Bible, and repeated the following words after Judge Sarah T. Hughes: "I do solemnly swear that I will faithfully execute the office of

President of the United States, and will to the best of my ability, preserve, protect, and defend the Constitution of the United States. So help me God." The new President of the United States leaned down and kissed his wife on the forehead. She took the hand of Mrs. Jacqueline Kennedy, who stood at the President's left and said, "The whole nation mourns your husband." The assassination had not only altered history, it had changed the places of the two women.

Mrs. Johnson had always gracefully accepted the fact that she could never compete with the glamour of Jackie Kennedy. She had acknowledged as much to close friends without any trace of sarcasm or envy. She had also expressed motherly sympathy for her young predecessor when Mrs. Kennedy, on first entering the White House, sometimes appeared unsure and unprepared for the role of First Lady. Now Mrs. Johnson grieved for her —and for the Kennedy family at their moment of deepest sorrow. She expressed her feelings on the telephone to the dead President's mother from the plane bearing his body back to Washington. She told Mrs. Rose Kennedy, "We feel like the heart has been cut out of us."

When *Air Force One* reached Washington and President Johnson had made his statement to a stunned nation, he said to his aide, Elizabeth Carpenter, "... go with Lady Bird and be of any help to her you can." As they were driving toward The Elms, then the Johnson Washington home, the new First Lady asked what she should expect. Mrs. Carpenter forecast accurately, "There will be reporters there. They'll want to know your reaction."

"The way I feel about it?" the shaken Lady Bird repeated. "It has been a dreadful nightmare, but somehow we must find the strength to go on."

"That's your statement," said Liz.

As Lady Bird took up a multitude of burdens including preparation to move into the saddened house at 1600 Pennsylvania Avenue, she urged Mrs. Kennedy to take all the time she needed to leave the mansion. Mrs. Johnson's sincerity was evident when she said, "I wish to heaven I could serve Mrs. Kennedy's comfort. I can at least serve her convenience."

There was another illustration of Mrs. Johnson's concern for those in trouble. When the morals charge against White House aide Walter Jenkins became public knowledge the same thoughtful Lady Bird sat down and wrote a statement of sympathy for the Jenkins family, which became the first official comment from shattered White House quarters. And while the pundits were speculating on possible political damage from the case, Mrs. Johnson went to call on Mrs. Jenkins.

When Lady Bird moved into the White House, she was generous in her credit to Mrs. Kennedy for the improvements that had been made, taking particular pains to point out to guests the changes and additions for which her predecessor was responsible. In due time, of course, the new First Lady put her own brand on the historic house—from the kitchen, where Zephyr Wright, the longtime Johnson personal cook was installed, to the collection of Doughty birds in the oval room and stacks of family albums and scrapbooks in the family sitting hall, to the rumpus room at the top equipped for gay, young parties. She added contemporary American art to the collection of paintings. She and the President recorded greetings to be played when tourists entered the mansion. She assembled a personal staff headed by Liz Carpenter, with Bess Abell as social secretary to help handle the heavy work load that accrues to being First Lady. But, as always, Lady Bird's first concern remained Lyndon B. Johnson.

A short time after her husband was catapulted into the White

House, Mrs. Johnson decided to try to do something about the breach between the North and her beloved South over civil rights. Her motivation at this time was more personal than political. She was saddened by the seeming estrangement of the area where she had her roots and where her kinfolk were legion. Discreetly she inquired about where she could go to make appearances that would not attract attention to the civil rights issue but at the same time would demonstrate that she wanted to try to help build bridges of understanding between the two parts of the nation. Quietly she began accepting engagements to speak on noncontroversial subjects that took her into the Deep South.

The culmination of this effort which turned into a political enterprise, as well, came in the middle of the 1964 campaign and was widely publicized. Lady Bird attempted what her tireless chief of staff, Elizabeth Carpenter, calls "the most dramatic campaign task any woman undertook." After much persuasion of LBJ, who feared possible political as well as personal incidents, Mrs. Johnson embarked on her own whistle-stop trip through the South in October 1964. She boarded the train at Alexandria, Virginia, and paused to explain why she was ". . . beginning . . . a four-day trip that will take me down the railroad track 1,682 miles to New Orleans. . . . I love the South . . . I am even more proud of the new South . . . I am proud of what the South has contributed to our national life. . . . We must search for the ties that bind us together, not settle for the tensions that divide us.

"A great Southerner, Robert E. Lee, said it best when he advised his fellow Southerners: 'Make your sons Americans.'"

Then she yielded to "the speaker in the family—my husband," and the President of the United States sent the train off on its healing mission—which was not diminished by an obvious purpose to garner votes, too. LBJ did not go along, although there have been times when a Lady Bird booking appeared to offer such promise that her husband decided at the last minute to make the trip also. This is said to have accounted for his sudden decision to go to Mexico in April 1966 for, as it turned out, something of a triumphal LBJ tour. His wife had pursued her Spanish lessons for what had originally been planned as a solo visit.

The requests for speeches by Mrs. Johnson run as high as 360 a month, only a tiny fraction of which can be granted. She has appeared occasionally on television. Although this medium tends to sharpen a face that is softer and more warm in person, nevertheless the image is that of a relaxed, gracious woman with a voice of pleasant modulation, the Southern accent toned down for a national audience. She received a coveted George Foster Peabody Award in 1966 for the program on which she guided viewers around the nation's capital on behalf of the beautification program. Lady Bird's husband can give the impression he does not care for serious family rivalry on television—or this may be to tease his wife. Anyway, a well-meaning visitor to the White House once remarked that Mr. Johnson could have some competition from the First Lady on the home screen. There was no comment as LBJ's attention was shifted to another guest. Later, he chidingly referred to the remark.

Lady Bird was soon aware that bringing their teen-age daughters to the White House was like asking them to live in a museum. But she was determined that neither girl should feel sorry for herself because her father was President. From an early age, Lynda and Luci were told of the importance of their father's work and their relationship to it. And although they once complained of being "de-privileged children" and often expressed the wish that they could see more of their mother, they accepted their lot. In the pre-White House days their mother, of course, was always at Lyndon's side—in Washington, on the campaign trail or on overseas trips as wife of the Vice President. It is estimated that she traveled 120,000 miles to 30 foreign countries in the latter role. When the girls were in grammar school, they spent half their time in Texas and the other half in the nation's capital. When in Texas, the family tried to rendezvous on weekends at the ranch, and Mrs. Johnson would go to Austin once a month to be with her daughters as well as to attend to family business at the radio station. The time spent with the girls was made an occasion for them to remember. There was one important compensation for Lynda and Luci in moving into the White House. They could see more of their parents than had been possible up to that time.

Of course, life in a goldfish bowl like the White House, with Secret Service agents accompanying the girls even on dates, was scarcely a normal life for either of them. At first, Lynda seemed to show some resentment over the public glare, and Luci wanted nothing to do with the political atmosphere. However, their mother wisely helped them to adjust to their surroundings. She soon could say that her daughters were wearing "their bonds rather lightly" and were very much at home in the world. Whereas Lynda had appeared to envy Luci's warmer, less self-conscious conduct in the spotlight, Mrs. Johnson found before too long, as she put it, "My girls like each other better all the time. As they grow older they grow closer."

Lynda arrived at the White House engaged to Lt. Bernard Rosenbach of Texas, a Catholic; but this relationship was terminated, and her most-publicized steady beau became actor George Hamilton, who introduced her to the Hollywood set and new ways of dressing and fixing her hair. Luci was graduated from the National Cathedral School for girls in 1965, became a Catholic that same summer, and in the fall entered the Georgetown School of Nursing. But Reserve Airman Patrick John Nugent, of Waukegan, Illinois, persuaded her to change her career plans, and on August 6, 1966, Luci became the eighth daughter of a President to marry while her father was in the White House. The nuptial Mass took place in the National Shrine of the Immaculate Conception, the largest Catholic Church in the United States, with a glittering reception afterward at the White House.

Lynda tends to take a historical perspective on life in the President's house. She has written, "You identify with history because you are there. . . . We are but the temporary tenants of 1600 Pennsylvania Avenue—this great house whose first occupant, Abigail Adams, wrote: 'This house is built for ages to come.'" Discussing the various reminders of America's past with which they are surrounded, Lynda recalled: ". . . Mother caught me studying late in the Oval Room, directly across from my room. She reminded me, rather firmly, that President Franklin D. Roosevelt had used this room as his study and that in the corner where I was working, Prime Minister Churchill had a desk where he went over reports on World War II until five o'clock in the morning during his wartime visits. I am sure Mother meant to discourage me from using such a historic room for my very unhistoric homework, but I told her that maybe the history would inspire me to greater work." *

Luci said in the spring of 1966, "The two most important things that have ever happened to me are my getting married and my conversion." † As for her mother, Luci wrote in the months before her wedding, "I'm closer to my mother. . . . We have so much in common; there's so much planning to be done

* "My Life in the White House," *Look*, May 18, 1965.
† *Seventeen*, May 1966.

for my marriage, and this is something that has to be worked on every day of the week." The First Lady cleared her calendar for June and July in order to devote herself to arranging "a wedding to remember always" for her daughter.

Lady Bird was once asked what she had found to be the most difficult part of her role. She confessed, "I think it may be the feeling of being under scrutiny, when really you would prefer not to care if your hair is windblown or your dress is the one you wore the year before last.

"It is the public attention you don't particularly want—to be on stage, to be looked at." *

However, she has adjusted to this demand of her public role with the same flexibility that has made it possible for her to adapt to the changes—often sudden and unexpected—which life with LBJ has always meant. She has laid aside the flat-heeled shoes and sports wear she once favored for understated up-to-date dresses that show off the youthfulness of her size 10 figure, always making sure that LBJ, who "passes swift and very frank judgment on my clothes," approves.

Whether in the White House, or at their ranch in Texas, no matter what kind of a day she has had, or what she may be involved in doing, the First Lady is always ready when she hears a masculine voice call, "Where's Bird?" Her response is, "Here, darling." That is her first place—and always will be. "This November we will have our thirty-first wedding anniversary," she wrote. "All these years have been spent in public life. Watching Lyndon in the Presidency, there is something a wife feels which is quite apart from devotion. It is deep compassion for the man who must cope with problems from Vietnam to Appalachia." †

* Josephine Ripley, *Christian Science Monitor*, September 17, 1965.
† "Lady Bird Writes Her Own Picture Story," *Life*, August 13, 1965.

3.

Mary Wilson—
United Kingdom

*T*HE pretty woman with golden-brown hair riding in the limousine through the gates of Buckingham Palace looked as proud as a queen but a little bewildered. The date was Friday, October 16, 1964, and Mrs. Harold Wilson was facing a dramatic transformation of her life. Queen Elizabeth had summoned her husband to the Palace to ask him to form a government. It was not in the usual tradition for a wife to be taken along on such an occasion, much less the children. However, as Mary Wilson explained later, "It wouldn't occur to Harold to do anything else." So she and their sons, Robin and Giles, waited in a reception room in the wings while Harold Wilson, by royal invitation, stepped onto the stage of history.

The mounting events of the previous hours had forecast this moment for Mary Wilson. Nevertheless, it was difficult for the onetime stenographer to accept the fact that the Oxford don

Wide World Photos

Mary Wilson

she had married twenty-four years earlier was turning into a Prime Minister. They had spent election night in Liverpool watching the returns from Wilson's constituency of Huyton and the rest of the nation. When it became apparent that the Labour Party had won—by a very small margin—they boarded the train for London. When she saw the policemen standing on guard in the corridor of their railway carriage, Mrs. Wilson had her first indication of coming events. The meaning of the vote began to dawn a little more clearly when they entered the dining car for breakfast. As she tells it, "There were camera lenses within a few feet of our faces. When the photographers asked him to put on this or that pose, Harold was cross and said he wasn't a performing seal and he didn't want pictures taken when he was eating...."

Arriving in London, they heard that Prime Minister Sir Alec Douglas-Home of the defeated Conservative Party had gone to the Palace—presumably to hand in his resignation. Mary Wilson "just felt light-headed." She went to their suburban home at No. 12 Southway Road in Hampstead because, she says, "I felt untidy and ready for a wash.... Only my hat gave me confidence.... It is customary in the Labour Party for women to wear red hats when they are electioneering. But I am a woman first and a politician afterwards and red doesn't suit me. This time, though, I found a cardinal style, cerise velvet hat with a stalk on top. Giles, my younger son, wanted me to cut the stalk off, because he said it looked silly—and it did catch in the car doors, but I liked it."

Even when a party member came to the house to get Harold's black coat and striped trousers, the full import of what was ahead did not register on the woman who would soon become mistress of the Prime Minister's residence at No. 10 Downing Street. But when she went to her husband's office in Transport

House, the party headquarters, and saw the detectives, she remembers, "I felt icy cold and there was a lump in my stomach."

It was four weeks after becoming Prime Minister that Harold Wilson and his family took up official residence on Downing Street. Mrs. Wilson said, ". . . I didn't want the Douglas-Homes to move in a hurry. I think it is uncivilized to rush these things and I said so." Although the Douglas-Homes left in three days, the Wilsons took their time about making the necessary household arrangements. There was considerable adjustment for the entire family. They had lived in the suburbs for sixteen happy years in a modest four-bedroom house with its array of bookshelves, comfortable reading chairs, and untidy sprawl of sports gear, mackintoshes and other impedimenta of two active boys. Their life was simple and withdrawn from the community. Once asked what type of things made her happy, Mary Wilson recalled a winter evening in Hampstead with the tea table laid, the curtains drawn, and a coal fire glowing in the grate. She was expecting her two sons. Giles, the younger, was due in half an hour and Robin in about an hour. She said dreamily, "It all looked very cozy when suddenly the door opened. Both boys came in, both early, together and smiling, and I found myself smiling, too."

In those days the Wilsons rarely entertained, nor were they gregarious socially or culturally, forgoing cocktail parties, dinners, concerts and the theater for evenings at home for what Wilson called "plain living and high thinking." In slippers he read biographies and historical essays with an occasional "guilty" sortie into a novel. He wrote speeches with the boys' radio "blaring dance music in the background." Mary read her favorite books—history, biography, novels with preference for the Brontës, Jane Austen, Thomas Hardy, Henry James and Dorothy Sayers, and the poetry of Keats and Tennyson. She also wrote poetry herself. Later, when she accompanied the Prime Minister on an official visit to Moscow, an excerpt from one of her compositions was printed in the Soviet press. It begins like this:

> After the bomb has fallen
> After the last sad cry
> When the earth was a burned-out cinder
> Drifting across the sky . . .

If she went out in the evening, it was usually to choir rehearsal at the nonconformist church to which the family belonged.

Now the time had come when political fortune forced the Wilsons to give up this simple, secluded existence for city life in a world spotlight. Their new home was a six-room apartment at the top of No. 10 Downing Street—above the reception rooms for official entertaining, which are over the offices, including the Cabinet room. Mary Wilson could not help telling a reporter, frankly, ". . . it isn't what I had expected. I thought I was coming to live in a house, but what we've got is a flat in a very big office building. The atmosphere is office, really. The flat goes with the job." (Kenneth Harris in *The Observer*.)

She recorded in her diary on Thursday, November 12, 1964, at five o'clock: "At last we've moved in. I've put all my pot plants in the sitting room and put up some pictures. When I get my books onto the shelves it should look more like a home and not just another hotel room, as Harold said. I found a beautiful bouquet of flowers from the people here at No. 10— a very nice welcome. Giles came home to tea and is starting his homework."

There were other aspects of her new surroundings that Mary Wilson could appreciate, like "being able to pop over to the House of Commons whenever I want to" and looking across the Horse Guards Parade from the small drawing room. And there was the intriguing ambience of the past which pervaded this eighteenth-century building that had housed so many famous figures. She told a reporter, "... of course, you're conscious of the history of the place. Portraits of Gladstone, Disraeli, Peel everywhere. You feel sometimes they're breathing down your neck—but I like that: you feel there's a steadying influence around you, and it gives you a sense of proportion."

Mary Wilson was quick to learn that the image of a suburban housewife which she had brought to No. 10, was not generally considered appropriate for the wife of the Prime Minister. There had been immediate publicity about her decision to fire the cook and take over preparation of the meals except for official entertaining, which she said would be catered by the government. She had announced that she needed only a cleaning woman who would come in for three hours every morning, observing, "We don't like having a staff around us in our home." She had brought along her electric washing machine in which she did the family laundry but used a dryer because she "couldn't see hanging out the washing at No. 10." She had continued to buy groceries at the cooperative, but by telephone instead of through personal shopping.

It was not long, however, before Mrs. Wilson told a reporter with some feeling that she hoped she had killed the "timid housewife image" which she felt was a bit unfair anyway. She explained defensively, "I consider myself reasonably well educated; I went to a good school. The idea that I am only interested in cooking and washing is ridiculous." She had found out that the Prime Minister's wife could not run the official household alone. She showed regret over the naïveté with which she had taken on her role and pique at the publicity given her first views. She attempted to put her position in a more appropriate light by admitting publicly, "Here, life is much grander [than in the little house in the suburbs].... Although a great deal is done for me here, I don't do the cooking and I don't do the cleaning and I do a great deal of official entertaining. I am not in the same sense my own boss because I have to ask a great many people or a great many people have to help me ... I was thrown in at the deep end, the day after we got here. I think I may enjoy it all in time. Parts of it I enjoy already. I don't mind the public dinners." (Kenneth Harris in *The Observer*.)

It was a major change for the daughter of a humble Congregational minister who had seldom entertained suddenly to be catapulted into the role of official hostess to the distinguished of the nation, the Commonwealth and the world. However, Mary Wilson's native ability to understand people behind veneers of title and wealth enabled her to make the adjustment. This is her formula:

> You can nearly always get on with people if you ask them questions about what they're doing, their work, where they've been recently, and that kind of thing, and I find that native curiosity gets you much farther really than trying to make "good" conversation. If I'm going to sit next to somebody who comes from a part of the world I know nothing about, I get somebody to try to tell me a bit about him or her, and after that I use my common sense.
>
> I don't mind public meetings, provided I don't have to make a speech. I don't mind being stared at, and I'm quite happy about being asked to get up and take a bow at a meeting—I don't feel awkward, or like a dummy. But I don't make speeches. Not even non-political ones. My heart sometimes gets very full, and that only makes it worse. [Kenneth Harris in *The Observer*.]

By comparison with his first margin of victory, Harold Wilson was given a handsome new lease on No. 10 Downing Street in the vote of the British electorate on April 1, 1966. From a

majority of three in the House of Commons he advanced to
ninety-two, and the greater political security was reflected in a
more relaxed atmosphere around the residence where social
activities increased. By this time, Mary Wilson was as much at
home in the house of the Prime Ministers as she had once been
in Hampstead, and she had accompanied her husband on official
visits to Rome, Paris, Washington, Ottawa, and Moscow. But
she never lost contact with the comparatively simple background
from which she came.

Gladys Mary Baldwin was born in Norfolk in 1916. She was
the only child of a Congregational minister who entered his
profession at twenty-nine after working in a mill from the age
of twelve and studying theology at night. His health was im-
paired by the starvation diet of stewed apples and rhubarb on
which he existed while preparing for his calling. Her mother
worked in the mill also until her fiancé entered the ministry and
they could be married. The Reverend Mr. Baldwin held many
pastorates, including Cambridge and Penrith on the border
of the Lake District.

Mary remembers her parents as "devoted . . . and very good,"
but "very strict, puritanical . . ." And they both were rebels.
Her father was a great reader, quoting the poets as often as the
Bible in his sermons. Mary was educated at a Sussex boarding
school—Wilton Mount—where the headmistress described her
as "not outstanding but quite a satisfactory pupil." She inherited her father's penchant for reading, and she recalls that when
she was at school "you were allowed to read novels three after-
noons a week. You drew them from the library and then you
returned them at the end of the afternoon. Apart from that,
if you were a compulsive reader, which I was, you had to read
and read your set books. Palgrave's *Golden Treasury* was the
only one I could go on reading. At one time, I practically knew it

by heart. I think that if anybody asked me if there was a book that had an influence on me, it would be Palgrave's *Golden Treasury....*" (Kenneth Harris in *The Observer.*)

Mary Baldwin studied shorthand and typing and then took a job with Lever Brothers in 1934 at Port Sunlight on the Wirral Peninsula. She was paid twenty-four shillings a week. Her "digs" cost one pound and insurance one shilling twopence. She was earning two pounds when she married.

An unforgettable memory may have influenced her interest in the Labourite who was to become her husband. "I'd seen the hunger marchers passing through Penrith. And then my father had done a spell at Hucknall, not far from Nottingham, where there was coal mining. It was before the days of pit-head baths. I used to see the miners go home black from the pits, spitting the coal dust from their throats as they went, to a bath in a tin tub in front of the kitchen fire, often as the children were coming in hungry from school. If I'd been able to vote at the age of eighteen I would have voted Liberal, and then in a year or two begun to vote Labour...." (Kenneth Harris in *The Observer.*)

Mary Baldwin and Harold Wilson met in Cheshire in 1934, when they were both eighteen. He had been born in Huddersfield, Yorkshire, the son of an industrial chemist, and attended school there until he was fourteen, when his family moved to Cheshire. He completed his secondary education at the Wirral Grammar School in Bebington, where he played cricket, captained the Rugby football team, and won a scholarship to Oxford. He was about to enter the university, and Mary was living away from home and working at Lever Brothers, when their paths crossed. Here is how it happened, according to Mary:

> We met at a tennis club. I was playing and Harold should have been home doing his revision for his Higher School Certificate. We'd both been going to the same Congrega-

tional Church, but he'd been going in the evenings and I'd been going in the mornings, so as a matter of fact we hadn't met there. . . . He had apparently decided to make me his wife three weeks after we met. . . . [Kenneth Harris.]

Five years later, a friend said she was surprised when Mary told her she was going to marry an Oxford don "because she looked only about fifteen. The following day, when Harold Wilson came for coffee, too, he looked about thirteen."

In 1937 Wilson won a first-class degree, one of the highest ever awarded at Oxford, and at twenty-one became one of the youngest dons at the university as a lecturer in economics. The following year he joined Lord William Henry Beveridge, the architect of England's "welfare state" as a Fellow of University College. Beveridge later described young Wilson as the ablest research student he had ever had.

The wedding date was set for January 1, 1940. Mary was at her parents' home in Lancashire preparing for the event when World War II broke out in September 1939. She moved to Oxford and took a job with the Potato Marketing Board. Harold volunteered for the Army, but with his growing reputation as an economist was drafted instead into the civil service. The Wilsons were married at Mansfield College, Oxford—the bride a fair, pretty girl in white lace dress, the groom with a round face described as "cherry-stone smooth," looked serious in the academic gown of an Oxford lecturer. Mary observed, "It was a Monday, the beginning of the week, the beginning of a new year, the beginning of a new decade, and the beginning of us. . . ." She told reporters, "When I married Harold I thought he was going to be a university teacher . . . and when Harold told me he wanted to teach at Oxford . . . I thought it was wonderful. My idea of heaven. I can tell you there's nothing I would have liked so much as being a don's wife. . . ." There was a short honeymoon in a hotel in the Cotswolds and then they returned to Oxford. However, Mary's hope for "heaven" was short-lived. Her husband was appointed to the Ministry of Supply in London and they moved to a flat in Twickenham.

As the London air raids increased and Harold Wilson was required by his job to travel to the unoccupied capitals of Europe and to Washington, Mary returned temporarily to Oxford, where she stayed part of the time in the home of the chemistry don at Jesus College and then with relatives in Cornwall. When she went back to London they acquired a flat at Richmond (on the Thames). She became an Air Raids Precaution Shelter Warden, wearing the regulation tin hat on tours of inspection at midnight and guiding people to shelters during the raids.

Their eldest son, Robin, was born in Westminster Hospital in December 1943. The following summer, when the buzz-bombing began, mother and son sought safety in the home of Mary's parents in Duxford, Cambridgeshire. They returned to London late in 1944. By Easter 1945 they were all back in Oxford, where Harold returned to University College as a don and his wife took up the kind of life she liked most.

The hope of Mary Wilson that at last they were settled was soon frustrated by politics. In July 1945 her husband was elected to Parliament in Labour's postwar landslide victory and became one of the three new Labour M.P.'s to go straight to the "front bench" in a junior ministerial position. In two years—at the age of thirty-one—he was the youngest man in a century to become a member of the Cabinet as President of the Board of Trade. Mary's duties were increasing, too, with the birth of Giles in May 1948. On February 14, 1963, one month after the death of Hugh Gaitskell, Harold Wilson was elected leader of the Labour Party. The following year he became the youngest Prime Minister since William Pitt.

Mary Wilson might have been a little more prepared for this sweep up the political ladder if she had pondered a childhood incident involving her husband. Eight-and-a-half-year-old Harold was taken by his father Herbert to see the British Empire Exhibition at Wembley. After a few hours of touring the fair, the Wilsons sauntered through Parliament Square and down Whitehall eventually arriving at Downing Street. The elder Wilson halted in front of No. 10 and took a picture of his son in his short trousers, schoolboy jacket, and cloth cap— posing on the doorstep.

The picture became a prophecy. And if there is one compensation above all others for Mary Wilson in its fulfillment, it is that she has "seen more of Harold Wilson since he became Prime Minister" than she had for years. Sometimes, this is only at breakfast, but there are occasional evenings together, since her husband tries to keep the official dinners down. And once in a while he "pops in" for lunch or tea.

Mrs. Wilson's day usually begins around seven when she arises and takes their Siamese cat Nemo down to the garden for his morning prowl. If Giles is in school, she prepares his breakfast, and then, tying a scarf around her head, walks with him to the underground. She enjoyed this jaunt particularly when she was not recognized—but now, of course, not only the sentries and police know who she is but an increasing number of the public. When she returns she has a cup of tea with her husband, who usually has read the papers and is finishing his breakfast. Then she checks on the household routine and goes over an enormous amount of mail. She frequently entertains at lunch. If there is time she may slip over to the House of Commons.

It was difficult for her at first when the opposition was rough with her husband. She told an interviewer:

> It's a terrible experience, until you get used to it. The worst time for me was when Harold couldn't make himself heard for nine minutes. You'd have thought they were going to tear him to pieces, like hounds baying for blood. I really came home very worried. Then that night I read that Asquith had been bayed at once for thirty minutes, and had to sit down with his speech unfinished, so I thought that in the circumstances Harold had got off rather lightly.
>
> Another thing is, of course, that you soon realise that it happens to everybody of any worth at all in the House. I was there once when they did it to Churchill. [Kenneth Harris.]

It is at night when the Wilsons have a chance to talk—even when the Prime Minister "is going through the papers in his red box"—the dispatch case with the latest cables and reports. If her husband is worried, Mary knows it by the way he walks up and down the room humming "a kind of tuneless, toneless, unrhythmic hum." Queried about what she did on those occasions, she replied forthrightly, "Ask what's on his mind. He always comes out with it. He's always ready to confide—but you have to ask him." Of course, she is sure he never tells her anything that is really secret. She recalls, "When he was President of the Board of Trade and I asked him what they were going to tax, he just replied, 'Inquisitive women, for a start.'"

Mrs. Wilson has some definite ideas about being a politician's wife. This is the way she describes them:

> I don't think a woman married to a politician should be a *political* wife. She mustn't try to push him. I know that some women married to politicians have been able to do a certain amount for their husbands' careers. If a woman

is ambitious she can do a great deal if she puts herself out to do it. . . . But after that he's on his own. And if he isn't capable of making the grade in himself, he won't get any farther. And if he isn't really up to it, and his wife is still prodding him on, he'll just crack up. . . .

She adds that in some cases women push their husbands "when, in fact, they are unconsciously competing with them— some women consciously compete with their husbands, of course." Mary Wilson long ago realized that "you have to decide. Either you go right in with your husband into all the activities of politics and put your children in boarding school or you make an agreed decision to concentrate on your home and children." She chose the latter.

When asked what she considered to be the most important quality for a Prime Minister's wife, Mrs. Wilson said thoughtfully that it was possessing "a sense of history." She explained:

> I was a little nervous at first at No. 10 Downing because it contained so much of the past, as if I might meet Pitt or Gladstone on the stairs. If you know anything about the past you know your own service is only a part of history and you are not likely to get either overanxious or overelated. It helps to keep one from getting swell-headed.

To keep their perspective and find rest and relaxation, the Wilson family goes as often as possible for weekends to the Prime Minister's country residence at Chequers Court, thirty miles from London. They like the fresh air and the walks in the woods, and Harold plays golf. Their favorite holiday spot is their bungalow in the Scilly Islands off Land's End. Out where the sea and sky meet, Mary remembers the morning she walked alone along the beach. The sun was just coming through the mist and the water was very blue and the sand was "white as far as you could see, and everything was very still and peaceful, but alive, very alive at the same time. Life without conflict. It was like the beginning of the world." Mary went swimming alone as she thought of the lines from Wordsworth's "Prelude":

> I felt the sentiment of Being spread
> O'er all that moves and all that seemeth still;
> O'er all that, lost beyond the reach of thought
> And human knowledge, to the human eye
> Invisible, yet liveth to the heart;
> O'er all that leaps and runs, and shouts and sings,
> Or beats the gladsome air; o'er all that glides
> Beneath the wave, yea, in the wave itself,
> And mighty depth of waters.

4.

Yvonne de Gaulle— France

YVONNE DE GAULLE has never revealed whether she was among the handful of dissenters in Colombey-les-deux-Églises when France voted overwhelmingly for a new constitution in September 1958. She is not one to confide in outsiders. But some villagers believe she used her ballot as a kind of silent protest against being uprooted once more from the rustic life they knew she preferred at La Boisserie in Champagne, her beloved manor house behind the lime trees at the edge of the woods. A new constitution meant that she and General Charles de Gaulle would be moving back to Paris and the politics, pomp, and pretensions she never liked.

De Gaulle had asked the people for a new charter of government with strong executive power. If he was to respond to their importunings to save France, with premiers rushing in and out of office as though through a revolving door, he needed ex-

Yvonne de Gaulle (left) with Patricia Nixon

panded authority. When the voters approved his constitution it was a forgone conclusion that Charles de Gaulle would be elected the first President of the Fifth Republic in December.

Regardless of how Yvonne de Gaulle voted on the constitution, she met the final verdict at the polls with her usual high regard for duty. In the tradition of her forebears she accepted the view that a Frenchwoman's home should be where the husband is, although her personal inclinations were more nearly described by the words of Sainte-Beuve, "to be born, to live and to die in the same house." Surrendering her own wishes, as usual, to the ambition of the man she had married thirty-eight years earlier, she put on her small black hat, climbed into the Citröen, and sitting rigidly behind the chauffeur, sped down the road to Paris. Yvonne de Gaulle was leaving behind the precious privacy of La Boisserie with its sweet-pea bed in the shape of the Cross of Lorraine which she had proudly created on the front lawn. She was sacrificing the joy of secluded drives in her two-horsepower car through country lanes and walks under the trees, and the right of a French housewife to shop personally for bread, meat, and cheese for her family. She was now to be First Lady of France and chatelaine of the historic Elysée Palace where Mme. de Pompadour had dallied with Louis XV and intervened disastrously in foreign affairs. By contrast with the eighteenth-century mistress of the King, however, the wife of the President would be zealous in maintaining Christian morals and observing the proprieties at the court of Charles de Gaulle.

The trip from Lorraine to the capital as wife of the President-elect was symbolic of the journey the former Yvonne Vendroux had made through the years from provincial obscurity to national prominence at the side of the man who became known as the savior of France. She might have anticipated as much had she taken seriously the words of a fortuneteller nearly half a century before.

On a gay holiday afternoon, several students from the proper Convent of St. Agnès in Asnières went to a fair where they consulted a clairvoyant. Looking at the hand of the prim, serious Yvonne in her uniform with its round collar and her hat with brim rolled back, the seer prophesied, "You will almost be a queen." (Curiously enough, this same prediction had once been made about Françoise d'Aubigné, who became Marquise de Maintenon, another Frenchwoman of great propriety.)

One of Yvonne's companions found the prediction preposterous. She asked sarcastically how one so shy and who cared so little for her appearance could reach such an exalted position. However, fate can confound logic. The shy girl did become "almost . . . a queen"—a First Lady, or the modern equivalent of the consort of a ruler. And there were those who said she looked like a queen. At a state dinner in Ottawa, as Mme. de Gaulle sat beneath the portrait of Elizabeth, the Queen Mother of England, other guests remarked on the striking resemblance between the two women.

Unquestionably Yvonne had much more to recommend her than the blessing of the occult when she first met the man who became almost a king. These were the traits a handwriting expert had read accurately in her neat penmanship: a sturdy character with energy, stability, integrity, orderliness, and conscientiousness. He had commented, "She is mistress of herself with a sense of responsibility and denies herself the pleasure of shining because of her great modesty."

Yvonne Vendroux, the second child and only girl among four children, was born on May 22, 1900, in the northern port city of Calais. The Vendroux antecedents, running back for two centuries, had been shipbuilders and cigar- and biscuit-makers.

One ancestor had fought with Lafayette in the American Revolution, while another had helped Simón Bolívar free Venezuela. Yvonne's father was president of a biscuit company. He had been in the consular service from time to time and directed many charities in Calais. Mme. Vendroux received the Military Cross for her services as chief of the nursing staff at the Calais military hospital in World War I.

As a girl, Yvonne divided her time, when not in school, between her Calais home and the Vendroux Château de Septfontaines in the rugged Ardennes, which she preferred. It was here that she first developed her lifelong love of flowers and the solitude of the forest. She was an excellent student in Calais and at the Dominican convent near Paris, where her inherited piety was nurtured. She was twenty when she met thirty-year-old Captain Charles de Gaulle. He also came from a deeply religious family which belonged to the anti-Republican Catholic Right, as did the Vendroux.

The de Gaulles had come to Paris from Normandy more than two hundred years before. The parents of Charles were cousins. Their backgrounds abounded in distinguished soldiers, lawyers, and historians. His father, Henri, was educated for the Army but turned schoolmaster to help support the family. In 1890 Charles's mother returned briefly to her home in Lille for the birth of her son on November 22. Soon afterward her husband became headmaster of the Jesuit College of the Immaculate Conception in Paris. Charles had three brothers and a sister. They lived in a large but modestly furnished apartment on the Left Bank. While not aristocratic or fashionable, they were eminently respectable representatives of the upper middle class.

The de Gaulle children were imbued from birth with the religious and patriotic fervor of their parents, who rated devotion to French history on a par with dedication to their religion.

The youngsters were induced to pore over records of the nation's past, and were shepherded to national shrines on holidays. One memorial in particular burned itself into childhood memories and probably helped to fuse passions for church and state into a mystical motivation for the future career of Charles de Gaulle. The Basilica of Sion near Nancy commemorated the fact that after the defeat of the French by the Prussians in 1871, patriots of occupied Lorraine and Alsace had laid on the altar a Cross of Lorraine broken in half. The inscription read: "Not Forever." In 1940 the fighting French under Charles de Gaulle remembered their unconquerable countrymen at Sion when they adopted the Cross of Lorraine as their emblem.

When Yvonne Vendroux first encountered Charles de Gaulle, he was already seasoned in the service of his country. He had received three wounds and four citations in World War I and had tried to escape five times from German prisons. Yet associates of the immaculate captain quipped that he came out of the trenches with his white gloves clean.

The meeting of the couple had been planned—but not quite the way it worked out. In November 1920, the Vendroux took their unmarried daughter to Paris to view the autumn Salon, *the* art show of the year. A friend who was not averse to matchmaking proposed that Yvonne should meet Charles de Gaulle and volunteered to produce the young officer at the exhibit. In a gallery surrounded by Braques, Dufys, Rouaults and Picassos, the far from avant-garde young people were introduced by the intermediary. The tall captain, whom fellow officers called "the long asparagus," and the shy young lady with "the wonderful gray eyes" sat down for tea. The conversation was strained. De Gaulle awkwardly balanced a fragile cup and saucer on his bony knee. Suddenly he shifted position and the tea splashed over Yvonne's dress. She laughed—and he decided she was pretty and charming.

The following day the correct officer, bouquet in hand, presented himself at the hotel suite where Yvonne was staying with her parents. A month later, while they were waltzing at the ball given by the students of the Polytechnic School, de Gaulle proposed and was accepted although Yvonne had earlier rejected other military suitors. During their courtship Mlle. Vendroux invited her fiancé to Septfontaines, where he hunted wild boar with her brothers. In the evenings, as they sat in front of a blazing hearth, the future President of France discoursed on history and philosophy. Yvonne listened attentively. When she did comment, her husband-to-be noted that she could hold tenaciously to a point and possessed a memory equal to his own.

Five months after they were introduced, on April 7, 1921, Yvonne and Charles were married in the Cathedral of Notre Dame in Calais. The bride who had once decided against being an Army wife now cheerfully accepted that role. She easily adjusted to her husband's career and agreed with his decision that they must live on his Army pay although her family had offered to supplement their income. The de Gaulles at that time established a frugal household economy that has continued through the years.

Yvonne's first home away from home was a tiny flat in Paris, rented while the captain lectured at St. Cyr and attended the French Staff College. Later, she set up barracks housekeeping in Trier and Mainz when her husband was posted with the Army of the Rhine. In 1930 their quarters were in a white Moorish villa in Beirut.

The de Gaulles returned to Paris in 1932 with three children: Philippe, named for Marshal Pétain, was born in 1923; Elisabeth in 1925, and Anne in 1928. Anne was their sorrow and their tenderest bond. She was retarded from birth, and during her twenty years of life could never speak properly, clothe, or feed herself. Yvonne's constant care of Anne over the years was augmented by a unique devotion of the father to the child. The officer who was austere with adults sat on the floor for hours playing childish games with the little girl, bouncing her ball, sailing her balloons, and singing nursery rhymes ridiculously off-key. Night after night he held her hand until she fell asleep. Anne died of a lung ailment in 1948. When her body was placed in a marble vault at Colombey, the Spartan General is reported to have said to his grieving wife, "Now at last our child is just like all children." Soon after her death, the de Gaulles established a home for handicapped children in the Chevreuse Valley, which is now sustained by royalties from the writings of Anne's father. However, in 1951 the institution was so desperately in need of funds that some consideration was given to mortgaging La Boisserie to save it. This was avoided when an able administrator rounded up the necessary financing. His name was Georges Pompidou.

Anne was an important reason why the de Gaulles decided to buy La Boisserie in the mid-nineteen-thirties. It offered the seclusion to provide the child with proper care and some outdoor life away from prying eyes. But there were other considerations. On returning from Lebanon, de Gaulle was assigned to the War Office, and the family rented a dark rear flat near Montparnasse. Cramped apartment living began to take its toll of family harmony. Yvonne longed for the gardens and woods she had known as a child—a place where she could put down roots. Her husband, increasingly frustrated by World War I military thinking in the government, carried his anger home and turned it into irritation against his wife. If she happened to be sitting in the gloomy dusk knitting and humming to herself—as she did frequently—the presence of guests never deterred a Gaullist outburst like, "Please, Yvonne!" A retired general has described an evening in the de Gaulle apartment: "Their flat was dark and the atmosphere somber. It was like entering an oriental household. The men would sit in one room, and the women would be whisked away by Yvonne. They would not be seen or heard all evening. According to my wife, they would knit and talk about their children's sore throats."

A fellow officer appreciated what de Gaulle's wife had to endure in that trying period when he said, "In those early days it must have been hell for Mme. de Gaulle. He was then very like the man he is today. That is to say he regarded himself as a superior being, above all contingencies. The difficulty was that whereas now he is President of the Republic, then he was an obscure colonel whose theories were largely ignored and who was disliked by most of the General Staff for his arrogance and rudeness. At home he was practically a tyrant."

De Gaulle's assignment was to the Defense Council which dealt with policies and planning in case of future wars. For five years—from 1932 to 1937—under fourteen governments he argued in vain that the next war would be a mobile, mechanized one and France must be prepared for it. He published a prophetic book on his ideas in 1934 that attracted some attention, so he concluded that he must do more to influence public opinion to his point of view. This called for a place to think and write. His mind was open to a home in the country.

On a fall day the de Gaulles came upon a small manor house with a dozen rooms in the Department of Haute-Marne about 150 miles from Paris. It was for sale. The building had once been used as a brewery and was known locally as *la brasserie*. But the town clerk had recorded it as "La Boisserie." They bought the property and added a square tower. At first, they spent only holidays and weekends at Colombey, keeping a Paris apartment for Yvonne and the children during school terms.

At La Boisserie, Yvonne had a place to grow her sweet peas, make jam, hang out the wash or spread it on the grass. There was space, fresh air, and privacy for the children. And her restless husband had his retreat for writing. De Gaulle described their home this way: "This part of Champagne is impregnated with calm, vast and sad horizons, nearby woods, cultivated fields and melancholy wasteland; in the distance stand the ancient mountains, time-worn and resigned. . . . Silence fills my house."

If the tower was the domain of the master of the manor, the rest of the house was under the firm rule of Yvonne. She never hung a "Visitors Not Wanted" sign on the gatepost, but she made it clear this place was primarily for her family. During all her years as First Lady only one official foreign guest has ever been invited to spend the night at Colombey. And then it took the President of France an entire week to convince his wife that the Chancellor of the Federal Republic of Germany, Konrad Adenauer, should be a guest in their home on his first visit to France!

Mme. de Gaulle was not able to make La Boisserie the full-time home of her entire family until a decade after it was purchased. Her husband's stubborn defiance of the establishment and the events of World War II were to delay fulfillment of this hope. In 1937 Charles was passed over for promotion and sent to Metz to head the 507th Tank Regiment. His advocacy of mechanized warfare was too much for the traditionalists who wanted to get him away from Paris. He spent his off-duty hours almost exclusively with Yvonne, who tried to interest him in card games in which she was an expert. Instead, he enlisted her help in preparing a new book, *La France et son armée* (*France and Her Army*), which was published in 1939.

If the French ignored de Gaulle's military foresight, the Germans did not. They occupied the Rhineland with two mobile divisions in 1936 and had twelve armored divisions by the time France got around to setting up two. French officialdom also failed to heed de Gaulle's warnings about war with Germany. When Hitler invaded Poland in 1939, the frantic officer defied the chain of command to send a secret memorandum to seventy-nine top officials, including Premier Édouard Daladier. De Gaulle declared that the Maginot Line was useless because the Germans would bypass it by air and mechanized armor. Daladier and other conformists were furious over a mere officer's arrogance. But when Premier Paul Reynaud came to power two months later he summoned de Gaulle from the front to ask him to draft a new defense program. However, Daladier was now Minister of Defense and he warned, "If de Gaulle gets in here, I shall resign." De Gaulle went back to the still passive front.

In the spring of 1940, when it became apparent that the Germans planned to drive through the Low Countries, de Gaulle was hastily promoted to Brigadier General—at forty-nine the youngest in the Army—and instructed to form and command the Fourth Armored Division. In spite of the inadequecy of equipment and preparation, de Gaulle's Division was the only unit in the Battle of France to delay the panzers and regain some lost territory temporarily. For this the General was cited in the Battle Order of the Day. Two months later, however, after the German victory, he was tried in absentia and condemned to death by a French military tribunal. His hero of World War I, Marshal Henri Philippe Pétain, had surrendered France to Hitler.

Yvonne de Gaulle had taken their children and Anne's nurse, Marguerite Potel, to La Boisserie when her husband went to the front. She had been given a private code by which he would communicate instructions if his worst fears for France were realized. On May 19—Yvonne's name day—the children were in the kitchen with Marguerite baking a cake for their mother when the gate bell jangled. The postman had a telegram directing the family to go immediately to the bedside of their Aunt Marie in Brittany. The cake was forgotten as Yvonne directed Mlle. Potel and the children to help her pack. The family sedan was stowed with winter and summer clothing as well as a few personal possessions including the General's collection of antique weapons. Three hours after the family and two dogs set off for Brittany, the Germans reached Colombey.

The next day the children were surprised to find their aunt in perfect health. Only Yvonne knew there was probably another journey ahead. Passports and directions to leave for England immediately arrived on June 16. She later learned that the tottering French Government that day scorned an offer of union with Britain which her husband had brought from Winston Churchill. De Gaulle recognized that capitulation to the Nazis was at hand when Marshal Pétain remarked, "What good is fusion with a corpse!" De Gaulle arranged to return to England that night by British plane after first sending the necessary credentials and instructions to Yvonne to follow.

The family set out for Brest on June 17, expecting to catch the next-to-last boat for England at one thirty. However, the car broke down en route to the port. Abandoning it and all of the luggage except for a bag of food which they called a diplomatic pouch, Yvonne crammed her charges into a borrowed two-seated conveyance and arrived at Brest in time to catch the last boat leaving for England for four years. The one they had missed was torpedoed and sunk two hours out in the Channel!

The passage took more than twenty-four hours as the captain

executed a zigzag course to dodge submarines and mines. At last they put in at Falmouth, where a banner on a kiosk at the dock announced: "De Gaulle Heads Free French." Yvonne quickly bought a newspaper which carried the text of her husband's first broadcast from London to the people of France declaring that French resistance would not be extinguished despite the surrender of Pétain. She told the children, "Papa is already at work in London. He is very busy. Perhaps we shall stay here for a few days and not disturb him." She settled them in a hotel room and then set about to trace her husband. She located him in a London flat loaned by a British friend. De Gaulle showed no surprise on hearing his wife's voice on the telephone. He merely said, "Ah, there you are. Take the next train to London, I shall be waiting at Paddington Station. There is a lot of work for all of you to do."

It is not clear whether Yvonne either wanted to or was expected to play a role in the Free French movement. A member of de Gaulle's London staff once remarked, "Though she was always fantastically loyal, I am sure Yvonne never understood what the General was up to during the war. Between ourselves, I don't think she approved of us Gaullists. She is rigidly conventional. We were military adventurers. In her heart of hearts she distrusted us."

Arriving in London, Yvonne discovered that her nearly penniless husband had undertaken to arouse a defeated country, raise troops, arms, and money with a single aide, while living in a three-room apartment that was to double as their home. For a while she took on the job of secretary until the British provided more appropriate headquarters for de Gaulle and a staff. After moving her family several times in crowded, bombed London, she settled them in a cottage in Ellesmere in Shropshire until the worst of the Battle of Britain was over, when they returned to the London suburbs. Philippe enlisted as a naval cadet and Elisabeth enrolled as a boarding student in the Convent of the Sisters of Sion. Mme. de Gaulle and Mlle. Potel, in the face of a slim budget and strict rationing, set about replacing the wardrobe they had all left behind on the road to Brest. Yvonne not only sewed and knitted for her own family but she also managed to turn out layettes for wives of servicemen. Her husband was adamant about observing rationing. Once Yvonne accepted an extra amount of milk for Anne. The stern father ordered the entire family to pool its coupons for the next week in order to repay the generous neighbor. He declared that English children were in the same plight and there must be no special privileges—not even for Anne.

Mme. de Gaulle kept house, queued up for hours to obtain food, and cooked. Her only relaxation came in sitting down to play a battered piano but with such results that her husband, home for a weekend, would complain, "Yvonne, that playing gets on my nerves." He preferred having her walk with him in the country, or sit with him as he edited speeches because he found her practical comments helpful. She also became his source of general news, clipping newspapers and magazines for items he might otherwise have missed. This practice became a part of Yvonne's daily routine, and members of the Presidential staff at the Elysée today are sometimes embarrassed by the "notices" she uncovers.

In the trying war years, de Gaulle leaned heavily on his wife as one to whom he could pour out anger and frustration over his lack of recognition. He recalled in his memoirs, "I had to cast myself in ice ... I was starting from scratch. Not the shadow of a force or of an organization at my side. In France, no following and no reputation. Abroad, neither credit nor standing ..." Although he continued to broadcast "in the name of

France," he was not accepted by many of his compatriots or by the Allies as the representative of the French Republic. President Franklin D. Roosevelt did not consider de Gaulle a full partner in the alliance and, therefore, did not even notify him in advance of the British-American landings in North Africa in November 1942. Instead, Pétain, then ensconced in Vichy, was asked for the cooperation of the French forces. The Marshal responded by ordering the troops in North Africa to resist. One officer who obeyed was the head of the Vichy naval forces, Admiral Jean Darlan, then visiting his son in Algiers. After three days of fighting, however, Darlan switched to the Allies and ordered a cease-fire in Algeria and Morocco.

De Gaulle was furious when he learned that the United States and Britain rewarded Darlan by naming him High Commissioner for North Africa. When Darlan was assassinated, Roosevelt and Churchill picked General Henri Giraud as successor, with de Gaulle in a subordinate role. In June 1943 the French Consultative Assembly, made up of representatives of resistance movements and various political parties, elected de Gaulle President of the French Provisional Government. He set up headquarters in Algiers and sent for his wife, Anne, and the child's nurse. Elisabeth was continuing her education at Oxford, and Philippe was on a Free French destroyer. In a villa in the suburbs Mme. de Gaulle became hostess to more guests than in any previous de Gaulle ménage. She suggested inviting the influential among the émigrés crowding Algiers, especially some of the more than one hundred generals who had deserted the Vichy regime. But her husband preferred intellectuals like André Gide and André Maurois.

De Gaulle, of course, was planning his return to France and training men who were ready to take over the liberated districts after the Allied landings. He arranged to lead the French troops into Paris ahead of the Allies on August 25, 1944, and set up in the Ministry of War the headquarters of the de facto government of France.

Sniper fire could still be heard in the streets when Mme. de Gaulle arrived in Paris with Anne. De Gaulle rented a private house for his family on the outskirts of the Bois de Boulogne in Neuilly. As Provisional President he refused to establish residence in the Elysée Palace because he said the cost of its upkeep was "inappropriate at a time of national austerity." The former Hôtel de Brienne was used for state entertaining where Mme. de Gaulle acted as an official hostess for the first time. One diplomat who was her dinner partner commented, "She is a woman who really listens; she doesn't discuss politics, but she has an extraordinary memory for people and events."

Yvonne remained in the background as much as possible, supervising four servants, including a chef and Anne's nurse, patronizing a neighborhood dressmaker for what gowns she needed for entertaining. She wore no makeup, and her hair was combed straight back with a knot at the neck. Her daytime jewelry comprised an engagement solitaire, a plain gold wedding band, and a brooch in the form of the Cross of Lorraine. Philippe was now fighting with General Leclerc in Alsace, but Elisabeth returned home. Although the girl had been on her own in England, she learned that in France her mother expected certain prewar proprieties to be observed. For example, when Elisabeth was invited to a victory luncheon in honor of young women who had served the Cross of Lorraine, Mme. de Gaulle said it was not proper for her to accept since she had not yet made her formal debut. On January 3, 1946, Elisabeth married Commander Alain de Boissieu, a graduate of St. Cyr, an early volunteer of the Free French, and a member of de Gaulle's military cabinet.

Charles de Gaulle had returned to France as a hero. He was treated as such for a time, but then the political factions began to look to their own interests. In early January 1946, Yvonne and her husband took their first holiday in seven years—at Eden-Roc, an elegant resort at Cap d'Antibes. There de Gaulle reviewed his position, about which he was becoming increasingly exasperated. As he said to his wife, those people were just impossible. They returned to Paris on Monday, January 14, and the Provisional President resigned the following Sunday.

The de Gaulles were ready to go back to La Boisserie for good—but it was not ready for them. Repairs of the extensive war damage were not completed because de Gaulle had refused to ask for a building priority. They rented the former royal hunting lodge at Marly, which was dank and cold from years of being unoccupied. It was also surrounded by guards. De Gaulle was assured these were for his protection, but later learned that he was really under surveillance because the new government feared a coup d'état.

In May they returned to Colombey, where Yvonne went to work on the Cross of Lorraine flower bed. When it was finished her husband showed it to a friend and said, "Some day when I die I will be buried here, and perhaps on this hill the government will see fit to raise a tall marble Cross of Lorraine—this is all the memorial I want." *

The General retired to his study to write his memoirs. His wife went back to her housekeeping and marketing in the village in her flat-heeled shoes and little black hat. They attended mass every Sunday, kneeling between two stained-glass windows depicting St. Louis and Joan of Arc. The priest said he could

---

* Alden Hatch, *The De Gaulle Nobody Knows*. Hawthorn Books, Inc., New York, 1960.

set his watch by the time of their arrival. After the death of their daughter they often visited her grave after church.

Elisabeth and her husband brought their little daughter Anne to Colombey, and Philippe and his wife came frequently with their three sons. Sometimes Yvonne would chide her husband for using barracks language in front of their grandchildren, and he would assure her that they did not understand it anyway. However, both of them were happy with young people around once more. But the General was restless, writing, "How many hours slip by in reading, writing, dreaming, when no illusion sweetens my bitter serenity." He anxiously watched a new decline of France as the politicians quarreled endlessly.

In May 1958, France was in ferment over the Algerian war. President Coty asked Charles de Gaulle to head a temporary government with extraordinary authority to stave off a grave emergency. He asked Yvonne what she felt he ought to do. Her reported reply sounded patly traditional, "My heart says No, but if your country calls, you must answer Yes." She saw vindication of her husband and a restoration of his morale in the offer. However, it was one thing to accept a six-month tenure in the Hôtel Matignon, the official residence of the Premiers, but it was something else to agree to a seven-year term in the Presidential Palace. And that was exactly where the interim service was to lead.

De Gaulle's niece has explained her aunt's attitude toward living in Paris. "It is a real privation for *Tante* Yvonne," Mme. Anthonioz has said. "Official functions are not amusing to her, for like my uncle, she loves family life. Also, she is a very good housekeeper, and likes to oversee her kitchen. Not to be able to run her own house is irritating to her. And she misses the garden and adores Colombey." *

* *Ibid.*

De Gaulle's principal objection to the official residence is that it lacks privacy. There can be no solitude in strolling through gardens surrounded by towering apartment houses, clubs and embassies.

Mme. de Gaulle first came to the Elysée two days before Christmas in 1958 to see her new "home." She was entertained at an elegant luncheon hosted by outgoing President Coty—caviar, cheese soufflé, glazed mandarin oranges. Afterward, she was escorted through the historic mansion with its thousands of pieces of antique furniture, two hundred tapestries, Sèvres china, and no less than 137 clocks. But she soon excused herself. It was obvious that this would be—as she said later—only a "furnished house" for them. She did not return until Inauguration Day.

This time she drove up in an unmarked car to the back entrance known as the Rooster Gate, because the ironwork is topped with France's national symbol. The butler was waiting to introduce her to the intricacies of the palace. When they came to the Presidential bedroom it was obvious that the General's oversized bed had not been delivered. Mme. de Gaulle briskly left, got into her car, and went back to the Matignon.

There she and the new President dined on cold cuts and salad and spent the night. Reluctantly they moved to the Elysée the next day.

The de Gaulles brought precise schedules and a stiff formality to the palace. They arise promptly at seven every morning, the First Lady awakening her husband because he does not permit a radio or any of the many palace clocks in his bedroom. At eight fifteen they enter the breakfast room for a meal which usually consists of bread, butter, and coffee with milk (except on Thursdays and Sundays, when there are croissants). On weekends at Colombey there may be a large omelette made from eggs laid at La Boisserie. The President is at his desk at nine o'clock. At this time Mme. de Gaulle begins conferring with the head chef and chief butler about household matters.

To avoid being seen, the First Lady then slips down a back staircase to the official rooms where she works with a staff in answering the mail that inevitably comes to a woman in her position. She knits for the poor, or embroiders the Cross of Lorraine on layettes and urges other official wives to do the same.

Promptly at one o'clock the President arrives for lunch in the small dining room. The hors d'oeuvres, meat, vegetables, cheese, and dessert are conveyed from the kitchens by dumbwaiter. Mineral water, red wine, and coffee are also served.

Like all other meals *à deux*, there is little or no conversation. As the President says, one goes to the table to eat. After lunch he rests for a time in solitude before returning to his office promptly at three.

Late in the day, Mme. de Gaulle may take her car (which is driven by a policeman, since she abhors bodyguards as much as does the President) to visit the fruit, cheese, meat, and pastry shops in the Madeleine section. Her selections are governed by her husband's tastes—those fruits and vegetables which are in season, plain cakes, English sweets, truffles, pork, *pâté*, quantities of tripe and cheese. She may stop at a department store or haberdashery to make a few purchases.

The President returns to their private apartment in the palace at eight o'clock to watch television news with his wife. Then there is a quiet dinner unless some official function is scheduled. They rarely dine out except with their daughter or son and grandchildren. Afterward, the couple may watch television again. The President prefers historical drama. The First Lady likes mild mystery programs. Both enjoy listening to singers. Occasionally, the General reads or plays solitaire while his wife knits or enjoys detective stories.

In March 1959, Mme. de Gaulle performed her first public function. She christened the new French jet airliner, *Caravelle*. About the same time she began to use lipstick and light makeup and to have her hair styled professionally. Designers encouraged her to help France's haute couture. She developed a taste for simple, understated fashions. Jacques Heim replaced her "little dressmaker," sending his wife and a model to the palace for the First Lady to make her wardrobe selections. According to Mme. Heim, "She is particularly fond of dresses with jackets or dresses with matching coats." She prefers a silk fabric, usually in tones of gray, beige, or black, which the General likes. She avoids green because of his distaste for the color, and when a sky-blue frock once caught her eye her husband cautioned, "Remember you're a grandmother." Her evening gowns have discreet necklines concealed further by stoles. Mme. de Gaulle does not bare her shoulders as Mrs. Eisenhower once did at a White House reception for the First Family of France. And foreign guests at the Elysée have been subjects of criticism when their attire has not been strictly in accord with Yvonne's code of the past. Queen Frederika of Greece and Princess Grace of Monaco did not escape private disapproval for their extremely modish ball gowns.

The conservatism in dress of the First Lady of France reflects a concept of morality and social conventions associated with the Victorian era. Divorced persons are not welcome in the official inner circle, and couples wed only in civil ceremonies are not enthusiastically received. Anyone suspected of unconventional living is not tolerated. President de Gaulle's renovation of the Grand Trianon, château of Louis XIV, at Versailles, as an official guest residence, with a sumptuous apartment for himself and Yvonne, is not expected to influence the First Lady toward a gayer and less restricted court life.

She is looked upon by many as the Mrs. Grundy of France, determined to save the morals of the nation in spite of itself. Her influence has been detected in a recent control over French literature, which has enjoyed, ever since Rabelais, the greatest freedom of language and subject matter. A subtle censorship of books is exerted under an almost forgotten law of 1949 which forbids the advertising or display of "publications of any kind that might endanger youth by reason of their licentious or pornographic character or their emphasis on crime."

Mme. de Gaulle is reported to have been shocked one day to find in her bookshop a titillating paperback on *l'érotisme au cinéma*. There was a storm at the Elysée until a legal basis could be found for action. Now the Sûreté Nationale, under the Ministry of the Interior, can bar from a catalog even the listing of any work that might offend sensitive modesty. Theoretically such a book can be published, but not offered for sale.

The First Lady is understood to disapprove of her husband's close friendship with his Minister of Culture, André Malraux. Perhaps she has heard that he once wrote an introduction for *Lady Chatterley's Lover*.

Of course, there is usually a chink in such an armor of conservative morality. The very proper Mme. de Gaulle is amused by the slightly off-color stories of the charming and intellectual Premier Georges Pompidou, who is her favorite in the official family. Possibly she developed some tolerance for this earthiness while reading to her husband when he was suffering from cataracts. His requests covered a wide literary repertoire and included many of the older French writers. Following successful surgery, the General resumed his own reading.

Mme. de Gaulle has also been known to question, tentatively

at least, one of the conventions with which she is burdened. She has privately acknowledged the boredom imposed by protocol that requires the same persons, regardless of congeniality or interest, to sit beside one another forever at state dinners because of the tyranny of rank. She has been known to whisper a hope that this rigid system might be made more flexible, but her disciplined conscience tells her that tradition must not be tampered with unduly, and she backs stiffly away from anything resembling innovation.

Whether La Boisserie holds the same ties for her today as it did in 1958 is a matter of conjecture. The President has indicated an increasing preference for Rambouillet, the official retreat, and for the Riviera for occasional weekends and vacations. And now there is also the Trianon. But there is little question of Mme. de Gaulle's action at the polls nowadays. When her husband was reelected for his second seven-year term in December 1965, registration was down, and so was the majority at Colombey. Out of 193 votes, de Gaulle received 175. An attempt was made to uncover the names of those who refused to endorse him. The secret service concluded that these were outsiders—engineers assigned to survey and keep up the roads into the village.

Mme. de Gaulle continues to hold her husband above all other considerations. She showed her mettle during an assassination attempt in August 1962. The de Gaulles were driving in Petit-Clamart, on the outskirts of Paris, when there was a sound of bullets. Two tires were punctured, causing the car to skid. The bodyguard sitting in the front seat cried out, "Duck, for God's sake!"

Another shot pierced the rear window and was embedded in the upholstery between the President and his wife. Neither flinched; both sat erect until the car stopped. Then they got out and calmly brushed the shattered glass from their clothing.

The General said, "They really are bad shots."

Mme. de Gaulle was asked if she was frightened.

"Frightened of what?" she snapped. "We would have died together—and no old age!"

5.

Carmen
Polo de Franco—Spain

*I*N the ancient church of San Juan el Real at Oviedo, Spain, a plaque marks the site of a "happy event" that occurred there on October 16, 1923. It was the wedding of a pretty, dark-haired daughter of a wealthy businessman to an ambitious Army officer from Galicia. At the time, the ceremony was of no interest outside northern Spain. In 1948, however, when the commemorative tablet was affixed to the wall near the altar, the occasion had acquired national historical significance. The inscription revealed that this was where "the Most Excellent Lady Carmen Polo de Franco" had married "His Excellency the Chief of State, Leader of Spain and Generalissimo of the Armed Forces, Don Francisco Franco Bahamonde."

On her wedding day twenty-five years earlier the bride had reason to believe that she was marrying more than an ordinary soldier. The Parish Register in the Sacristy recorded the

Carmen Polo de Franco with her granddaughter, Maria

fact that King Alfonso XIII and Queen Victoria Eugénie were sponsors of the bridal couple. This was a courtesy extended to an officer who had attracted the attention of his sovereign. Lt. Col. Francisco Franco, cofounder of the Spanish Foreign Legion, had been given the honorary title of Lord of His Majesty's Bedchamber for distinguished military service. Basking in royal favor, he had availed himself of the right to ask Alfonso to be best man at his wedding. The King designated the military governor of Oviedo as his stand-in. Ironically, Franco later made himself the stand-in for the monarchy, endowing Carmen with a status that was most congenial to her background and inclination.

Carmen Polo y Martinez Valdes, the oldest of four children, was born in 1898 in Oviedo, which had been a royal city for centuries. This capital of the province of Asturias, lying between the Cantabrian Mountains and the Bay of Biscay, was the seat of the Visigoth monarchs and the Kings of Asturias. In more recent Spain, the eldest son of the King carried the title of Prince of Asturias. Carmen became deeply attached to her monarchical environment. She also developed a concomitant devotion to the Catholic Church, encouraged by her devout parents and the Silesian nuns at the convent where she attended school. As a sheltered daughter of a strict Spanish family she expected social restrictions and heavy chaperonage until she married. But this supervision became irksome to Carmen at fifteen when she met an officer at a dance. He was twenty-three-year-old Francisco Franco, member of the glamorous Prince's Regiment and the youngest major in the Spanish Army.

Franco was born in 1892 at El Ferrol, the northern seaport of the province of Galicia, next door to Asturias. His father was a naval paymaster and his mother the daughter of a commandant. He hoped to follow his older brother Nicholas into the naval academy but enrollment was closed by government re-trenchment following the Spanish-American War. Nicholas eventually became an Admiral, while Francisco embarked on an alternate course through the Army—enrolling in the military academy in Toledo. On graduating, he took the soldier's oath to defend with his life the united Spain won by the Catholic monarchs, Ferdinand and Isabella. He volunteered for overseas duty and distinguished himself in battle against the Rif tribes-men in Morocco. However, brashness rather than bravery brought him to Oviedo, where Carmen Polo lived.

Captain Franco was critically wounded in 1916. He was awarded a coveted decoration but was refused a promotion he believed he deserved. Feeling that his superiors were being un-fair, Franco took advantage of a privilege available to any officer and appealed directly to the King. Alfonso resented attempts by the military high command to curb his authority, so he was delighted with any opportunity to assert it. He ordered that Franco be advanced to major and assigned to the Prince's Regi-ment in Oviedo.

Brown-eyed Carmen, with hair falling to her shoulders, was the envy of her friends when Franco began showing her atten-tion. It did not matter to the young romantics that the officer was older and shorter than Carmen. Francisco had military status and the one quality above all others admired in Spanish men—physical courage bordering on contempt for life. However, Carmen's father was not impressed. He told his daughter that she came from one of the best families of Asturias and therefore should be able to find a more worthy suitor than the son of a villager of Galicia. Señor Polo also objected to Franco's pro-fession. Years later, Carmen explained why. She said, "In my home we were all pacifists. My father warned me against marrying a soldier because at the first sound of a shot he would be off, leaving me alone."

It became apparent that neither parental objection nor class nor age difference could stay the course of romance. Franco's associates noticed a marked change from the man who in Africa had never dated or attended mass. Carmen cooperated with Francisco in evading restrictions of family and mores to meet clandestinely—often using the church as a place of rendezvous. Three years passed and Franco was not able to win over Carmen's father. Then duty intervened and he was posted back to Morocco. Before leaving he told the young woman he was determined to marry her and that he would return in a position that her father could not ignore. He would fulfill an old Spanish saying, "A *Gallego* [man of Galicia] knows how to wait."

In October 1923 Lt. Col. Francisco Franco came back to Oviedo to claim his bride. He was now adjutant to his good friend, the commander of the Spanish Foreign Legion, General Millan-Astray. The nuptial mass was celebrated and, according to Carmen, her father began "following, on the maps, with passionate fondness the course of the African war in which Franco was participating." After the honeymoon Carmen remembered her father's warning about being left alone if she married a military man, so she accompanied her husband to Morocco. There she first came into direct contact with his authoritarian control over others and the code of severity practiced by Spanish military men toward subordinates. By royal intercession Franco was soon advanced to General—the youngest in the Army—and Carmen became the social arbiter of the small select set in which they moved. Their only child, Carmencita, was born in Morocco in 1927.

The Franco family returned to Spain in 1928, when the General organized the military academy in Zaragoza, capital of Aragon, and became its principal. He was sent to France to study under Marshal Pétain at the St. Cyr Academy, and to Berlin and Dresden to become acquainted with the new, improved German military system. But the reign of the royal patron of the Francos had begun to run out. Its end was to have a far-reaching influence on the future of Carmen and her husband.

The Bourbon Monarchy entered the twentieth century with little authority and tarnished prestige in a Spain humiliated by the outcome of the war with the United States. Alfonso XIII had to lean on the Army to stay on his shaky throne. To please the officers, he pressed Parliament for large sums for campaigns in Morocco, their only military outlet after the loss of Cuba and the Philippines. The Army became a political power to be reckoned with. In 1917 it protected the monarchy by breaking revolutionary strikes which reflected unrest over the losses in Morocco as well as a stirring of republican sentiment.

The military saved Alfonso for the last time in 1923. He had been publicly linked to a disastrous defeat in Morocco two years earlier, and it appeared that his ruling days were numbered, as his coalition cabinets became impotent. Then General Miguel Primo de Rivera y Orbaneja seized power in a military coup and established a dictatorship with the blessing of the relieved monarch. Small sprouts of constitutional government which had been struggling for life were virtually smothered under the General's exercise of personal power. Inefficiency and corruption flourished along with prosperity.

At the end of 1929 the world depression reached Spain and contributed to serious economic problems for the country, which also faced separatist unrest among the Catalans. Alfonso decided to dismiss Primo de Rivera and to experiment with substitutes. On April 12, 1931, municipal elections which were comparatively free of irregularities showed a strong tide running against the monarchy. The King inquired discreetly whether he could count on the Army, as in 1917, to save him. When he learned that the answer was No, he quietly slipped out of the country on the night of April 13, 1931. The Second Republic was born the next day.

The new regime began immediately to prune the officer-heavy Army. Franco's military academy in Aragon fell under the ax. In his farewell speech to the cadets, the principal did not hide his monarchist sympathies, but he did advise obedience to the established order "even when it is in the wrong." An irritated War Ministry reacted. It reduced Carmen's husband to an infantry brigade commander and stationed him in the northwest at La Coruña and then he was posted to the Balearic Islands in the Mediterranean. During this period, Franco tried to enter politics by running for a seat in the Cortes as a monarchist, but failed.

The prospects for Franco's career brightened again in 1933, when there was a Rightist Catholic victory at the polls. He was called to Madrid to be Chief of Staff, where he gained a reputation for brutality in suppressing discontent. The political trend that reversed the Franco fortunes heightened unrest and protest in Carmen's native Asturias and in Catalonia. When the Asturian miners openly revolted in 1934, Carmen's husband ordered in the Foreign Legion and Moorish troops. The use of Moors in Spain was without precedent. The slaughter earned the Chief of Staff the title of "butcher." When the Popular Front, formed by moderates and Leftists, took over the government in 1936, Franco was remembered for the excesses in Asturias and banished as commander to the Canary Islands off the northwest coast of Africa.

This is Carmen Franco's version of what happened:

> We were in Madrid where my husband held a high military post to which he had been appointed in 1935 by the then Minister of War, Señor Gil Robles. His was the highest military rank a soldier could ever achieve and my husband held it at a comparatively young age. He was only forty-three.
>
> We were happy and contented. Then came the triumph of the Popular Front at the elections in February 1936 and my husband was distrusted by members of the radical cabinet.
>
> The result of this distrust was a ... post as head of the military command at the Canary Islands. He was a soldier and so obliged to go wherever he was sent. And off we went to the Canary Islands.

The Francos lived in the official residence of the commandant between a large banana plantation with volcanic peaks as a backdrop and the Atlantic Ocean off Santa Cruz de Tenerife. The General took up golf and, since he had plenty of time on his hands, decided to study English also. He received lessons three mornings a week from a teacher in Tenerife and wrote six exercises a week for his homework. Five of them were usually about golf. However, life for Doña Carmen was anything but carefree in the Canaries. She has explained why:

> There we knew anguish. I did, especially, because my husband is most courageous and fears nothing.
>
> His adjutants came to me one day and told me there was a plot against my husband's life. He knew about it but didn't care. They wanted my permission to create a permanent guard that would follow the General wherever he went—unknown to him, of course, because he never would have stood for it.
>
> I agreed. Then came days when we would go here and there—never knowing where or when death would strike.

Carmen was concerned for the safety not only of her husband, but also for Carmencita and herself as threats were directed against the entire family.

If Carmen's husband was the object of a plot, he was also participating in a military conspiracy to overthrow the republican government in Madrid. When the leader of the Monarchist opposition in the Cortes, Calvo Sotelo, was murdered on July 13, 1936, the cabal seized on the incident as an excuse to speed up its plans. Secret orders went out to the military commanders to strike on the night of July 17—and launch the civil war that was to torture Spain for three years, cost one million lives, and give Fascists and Communists a proving ground to try out their weapons for World War II. General José Sanjurjo, a Carlist living in exile in Portugal after attempting an abortive military rebellion in 1932, was to head the uprising. But his plane crashed just beyond the runway at Estoril as he was taking off for Spain. Manuel Goded, Captain-General of the Balearics, then stepped in by flying to Barcelona. He was arrested and executed.

Meanwhile, Franco had been making his plans on the Canary Islands. The death of the military governor of nearby Las Palmas, General Amado Balmes, fitted nicely into them. He asked the War Ministry for permission to attend the funeral, which was granted. At 12:30 A.M. on the morning of July 17, General Franco, carrying a small valise in which there was a black suit, took his wife and daughter aboard an interisland steamer for Las Palmas. When the funeral was over, Franco in his black suit with his uniform in a brown paper bag went to the airstrip where—by prearrangement—a chartered British plane was waiting. He told Carmen he was going on an inspection tour of the islands and was soon airborne. In flight, he changed into his general's outfit. After spending a night in Casablanca he landed at Tetuán at dawn on July 19 and took command of the revolt in Morocco.

By this time, Franco's mission was well known through a manifesto which he had issued. It called on all Spaniards, especially those in the armed services, to rise up against anarchy. He declared:

"The pistol and the machine gun annul the differences between groups of citizens who are maliciously and treacherously assassinated without the public authorities imposing peace and justice." Franco arranged through Hitler and Mussolini for Nazis and Italian Air Force planes to fly Moorish troops and Foreign Legionnaires into Spain—some of them strapped to the wings—and then arrived on the peninsula himself to restore his own particular brand of law and order.

When Carmen parted from Franco in Las Palmas, one of the General's aides handed her instructions left behind by her husband. She followed them by taking, with Carmencita, a boat bound for France. From here they eventually made their way to Portugal, where they could enter western Spain and join the General in Cáceres in September. They followed him to Toledo and then to Burgos, capital of Old Castile, which had become the insurgent capital. There Franco's political maneuvering and his reputation as a successful military man combined to push him into acknowledged leadership of the group of generals running the rebellion. The junta adopted a decree on September 29 designating him "Head of the Government and Military Operations" and the investiture, in the presence of Carmen and Carmencita, took place the following day in the throne room of the gray-walled palace. Franco responded with the hardly modest assurance to the junta: "You have placed Spain in my hands, and I assure you that my hand will not tremble. With your help I will raise Spain to a lofty height, or die in the attempt." In Franco's first decree he referred to himself as "Head of the State."

As the civil war raged into 1937, with Spaniard slaughtering Spaniard, Doña Carmen found life rather normal in the Franco household, which was then established in the Bishop's palace in Salamanca. She wrote in a newspaper article for worldwide distribution:

> Our life now is not much different than the life we have always led. My husband gets up in the early hours of the morning—seven or seven-thirty, and works constantly—sometimes until two or three in the morning.
>
> My husband's favorite pastime—reading—is not entirely forgotten. If he ever gets a free moment he spends it with his books, mostly dealing with military matters.

There was no doubt in Carmen's mind that her husband was right in his methods as well as his goals. She declared in her press piece:

> I have absolute confidence in my husband's ability to carry through to a victorious triumph this movement he started, prompted by his ardent patriotism.
>
> He loves his military career—has given all his life to it. And I love it as much as he. A strict disciplinarian, a stern believer in duty, he served the Republic as faithfully as he had served the Monarchy, disregarding personal preferences or ideals. But above all stood his love for Spain. I've seen few men who loved their country as deeply. It is almost a "cult" with him.

The wife of the Generalissimo not only approved what her husband was doing, she discovered the usefulness of the Bureau for Press and Propaganda in promoting his aims. She collaborated in arranging a national appeal signed by little Carmencita to all other nine-year-olds "to pray for peace and Papa's victory."

In 1938 Carmen witnessed in the historic twelfth-century convent of Las Huelgas, one mile southwest of Burgos, where many Castilian kings and queens are buried, confirmation of the expansion of her husband's assumption of power. In the lofty stone hall hung with tapestries presented by Alfonso VIII and his English Queen Eleanora, Spanish Cardinal Gomar pronounced Francisco Franco "Head of the Spanish State and Prime Minister." Shortly afterward, Franco assumed the title of Caudillo de España por la Gracia de Dios ("Leader of Spain by the Grace of God").

The new Cabinet included the husband of her sister Zita—Serrano Suñer (an ardent Nazi supporter)—as Minister of the Interior. He was later to become Foreign Minister. Carmen's brother-in-law described the oath-taking ritual as "intimate, fervent, and devout, like a vigil in arms." Later in the cloister the nuns served sherry and traditional wafers made with egg yolk, suggesting a royal rather than political occasion.

It was well over a year later, however, before Franco could offer Doña Carmen and Carmencita a royal home in Madrid. At last, on April 1, 1939, there was unconditional victory for his million Spanish troops augmented by Italian Fascists, Nazi technicians, and hundreds of German and Italian planes, tanks, and trucks. They had battered down the Republicans, who were aided by Russia and international volunteers. Spain was a torn and bleeding preview as the rest of Europe now prepared for World War II. Hitler pressed the Spanish dictator for help in return for his help in the civil war. The Caudillo agreed to one division for use against the Russians, but he denied passage through Spain to troops of either the Axis or the Allied powers.

As the Spanish people began trying to rebuild their shattered lives and nation, their new ruler decided that the appropriate residence for him and his family was a royal one, El Pardo Palace, which had once been owned by the Prince of Asturias. The white granite structure with its pointed towers and steep tiled roof resembling a French château is located some fourteen miles northwest of Madrid on the site of a hunting lodge once used by Philip II, to whom Franco is often compared. The formal gardens and forests amply stocked with game for the master's shooting pleasure slope gently to the Manzanares River teeming with fish for his catch. The setting, backed against the Guadarrama Mountains, has been captured on canvas in royal hunting scenes by Velázquez and del Mazo.

When Franco decided that El Pardo would be their residence, he went out to the palace with two Madrid architects. They proposed elaborate improvements. The Chief of State listened and then, after his usual moment of silence before uttering an opinion, said, "Be sure that all the windows and doors really shut." Doña Carmen suggested that there be added a swimming pool, tennis courts, a golf course, and a "little cottage" removed from the palace proper. In this kind of Petit Trianon her husband can withdraw to read, rest, and be alone. Franco gave up tennis some time ago but still plays golf, hunts, and fishes at El Pardo and the summer palaces in the north, where the family spends one month each at El Pazo de Meiras in La Coruña and Ayete in San Sebastián. A high gray wall was built around El Pardo to screen the grounds from unauthorized access and public view.

In 1947, Doña Carmen's husband moved closer to a monarchical role that was particularly pleasing to them both. He assumed the title of Regent and arranged for a Law of Succession that created a Regency Council to decide on his successor as a "person of royal blood. . . ."

Doña Carmen presides over an appropriate court setting at
El Pardo with its treasures of the Spanish masters, Goya tapestries, and Aubusson rugs. She readily enters into pseudo-royal
pageantry. When she appears on a formal occasion, the "Queen's
March," hitherto reserved for royalty, is played on order of her
husband. At a special ceremony like a charity function, a benefit
bullfight, or the saying of a pontifical mass at a Eucharistic Congress, she occupies a raised dais not unlike a throne. In a black
Balenciaga gown with ever-present pearls, her handsome head
held proudly, the First Lady of Spain strives to look every inch a
regal patroness.

Señora Franco trained Carmencita to conduct herself like a
daughter of royalty. As a teen-ager, the girl was taught to pre-
side over functions for poor children and visit worthy institu-
tions, as Elizabeth of Britain did when she was a princess. When
the Franco heiress married the Marquès de Villaverde, a heart
surgeon, at a glittering ceremony in Madrid, she wore a diamond
diadem. Carmencita's mother accompanied the young couple on
a honeymoon pilgrimage to Rome, where they sat at the left of
the papal throne to attend the canonization of the Spanish St.
Anthony, a textile worker who became Archbishop of Cuba
over one hundred years ago.

Doña Carmen's attraction to royalty extends beyond the
house of Franco—or Bourbon. When a Spanish girl became
engaged to King Baudouin of Belgium, she visited the future
Queen Fabiola in her Madrid home and gave her a wedding
gift of a gold-and-platinum crown.

Franco expects formal deference for himself that suggests behavior toward a monarch. At religious rites he invokes a royal
prerogative by walking under a canopy. Civilians received at El
Pardo wear morning attire with striped pants and the military
appear in dress uniform. New ambassadors in full court regalia

arrive in gilt state coaches and pass between mounted guards. At a state dinner the guests file in front of a dais where the host stands with uplifted arm.

Some people believe that Franco was thinking of his successor when he had special legislation approved to permit the older of his two grandsons to bear the name Francisco Franco, instead of the surname of the child's father. If that idea is in the mind of the aging dictator, he has also taken care to keep hope alive among the heirs of Alfonso. And to this end he has engaged the natural interest of his wife in the subject.

Doña Carmen went on a special mission to Portugal in March 1958. She had three—some reports say four—meetings in Lisbon and the Madeira Islands with Don Juan, third son of Alfonso XIII, and outstanding pretender to the throne. News dispatches said she called the pretender "Your Majesty" and curtsied deeply. Two years earlier, when Don Juan learned that Carmen was passing through Estoril on her way to Madeira for a holiday, he had invited her and the Spanish Foreign Minister to tea. When the grandson of Alfonso XIII, Prince Juan Carlos, visited El Pardo after arriving in Madrid to attend school, he was met at the palace gates by the First Lady of Spain, who swept into a deep curtsy.

Despite the referendum of December 1966 the question of the succession remains unresolved—except possibly in the mind of the man who rules Spain today. Meanwhile, the private life of the First Family proceeds simply in the many-splendored palaces. Here the stern Caudillo unbends and acts like a doting grandfather toward the seven children of their daughter Carmencita. His wife calls her husband Paco, the usual Spanish diminutive for Francisco, and plays the multiple role for which she feels she is best qualified—wife, mother, and grandmother.

Doña Carmen usually begins her day with mass in the private

chapel of the palace. If it is Sunday or a feast day, her husband joins her at morning prayers. When traveling the two seek out a church for religious service on reaching their destination. An aide has explained, "They have much to give sincere thanks for, and they never fail to give them." Carmen receives official visitors in the morning and then lunches with her husband and any of the grandchildren who happen to be around. Sometimes they are joined by her bachelor brother, Felipe Polo, who serves as social secretary to Franco. In the afternoon she visits old friends or goes shopping, sometimes with her oldest granddaughter. She enjoys antique shops and visits to art galleries and concerts. She lends her name to worthy charity functions and will make a public appearance on behalf of a cause in which she is interested, particularly if it is sponsored by the Church. She is known to the American Women's Club in Madrid, where she occasionally appears.

Doña Carmen has described the family evenings this way: "Every night after dinner, if there is no official function, the Generalissimo and I sit quietly at home, reading and relaxing. My husband does not smoke or drink, except for an occasional glass of wine with dinner. Then, too, every night there is the matter of arranging the next day's menus. When we do not have guests, this is an easy matter, for our tastes are very simple. We both eat everything." (Neither of the Francos is a gourmet, and some of their fare is as simple as tasteless soup and fried fish.) The evening may be topped off with watching a moving picture in the projection room, with Franco sometimes screening his own work like any shutter fan.

About midnight, Doña Carmen kneels with her husband to say the rosary. The Caudillo keeps a precious religious relic, the mummified hand of St. Teresa of Avila, in a silver case on the reading table at the head of his bed. St. Teresa was made the revered patron of the Army Service Corps, on the initiative of Alfonso XIII. One of the saint's well-known sayings is, "God is also found among the pots and pans."

Franco's final prayer before retiring is one of his own composition: "Lord who entrusted Spain to my hands, do not deny me the grace of handing a Spain back to you which is truly Catholic."

Doña Carmen watches carefully over her husband's well-being and has taken thought shrewdly for the future. She is an excellent businesswoman and a belief persists that she has demonstrated this skill by making substantial investments in real estate in Madrid as well as outside the country, particularly in Switzerland. Another report which has been current for some time is that she has acquired and furnished luxuriously a residence on Madeira, "the island of the gods," which belongs to Portugal—in case her husband's retirement should require it.

Francisco Franco has also been planning for his future. In the grand manner of Philip II he has built into the Guadarramas near Madrid, where the rebel columns were stopped during the civil war, a vast memorial known as the Valley of the Fallen. On either side of an enormous chapel rivaling St. Peter's, surmounted by a huge cross that can be seen for miles around, there are catacombs for the final resting place of the heroes of the civil war. And the greatest of these heroes in the eyes of the woman who lives at El Pardo is Francisco Franco.

Jovanka Broz Tito

6.

Jovanka Broz Tito–
Yugoslavia

HE President of the United States turned
to the exuberant brunette in modish black suit, diamond earrings, and pink hat sitting in the place of honor at his side and
said she must be proud of her fighting record.

This conversational gambit would have sounded ridiculous to
an uninformed eavesdropper at the White House luncheon on
October 17, 1963. But it was natural for John F. Kennedy to
put the question to Jovanka Broz Tito, wife of the Chief of
State of Yugoslavia. She had once been a guerrilla soldier in the
mountains of the Balkans, shouldering a rifle along with the
best of the defenders of her homeland.

Yugoslavs have always lived at a geographical crossroads that
has been contested many times through history. This fact of
Balkan life is illustrated by a story that was told throughout
the country after World War I.

It seems that old King Peter I of Serbia met an anguished peasant searching the battlefield. He asked if he could help. The sorrowing subject shook his head and said, "I'm afraid you can't. I have already lost five sons in Balkan wars, and now I am looking for the body of my sixth and last one." The more Peter tried to comfort the bereft parent, the more the King seemed to be making excuses for asking such a sacrifice. "Oh, I don't blame you for the misfortune that has come to me," explained the peasant. "If anyone is to blame it is our ancestors who settled here hundreds of years ago. Why did they choose the Balkans? The whole world either wants the place or wants to go through it on the way to somewhere else. *That* was the great mistake."

Nazis and Fascists were trying to go through Yugoslavia in 1940, when sixteen-year-old Jovanka Budisavljevic joined the Communist underground. With her usual energy she began to organize a resistance movement among the peasant youths in her native Croatia, holding meetings in her modest home and exhorting everyone to join in the fight against the invaders. She revered the memory of a young Communist of the Lika district who had died at the beginning of the war, Stefan Matič. She put flowers on his grave and solemnly recited poetry in his memory. When the people of her village of Pecane told an interviewer later that Matič was Jovanka's first love, the woman who had now become the wife of Marshal Tito denied the allegation and explained, "Stefan Matič was a young Partisan leader of my area. Yes, I did lay a wreath on his grave and recite a poem dedicated to him, but I never knew him. He was a Partisan hero, a symbol. I was deep in communism, a terrain worker, a secret indoctrinator, long before he died." *

Jovanka enlisted as a private in the Partisan army in 1942.

---

* Helen Worden Erskine, *Collier's*, October 2, 1953.

Louis Adamic, the Yugoslav-born American author who was sympathetic toward the Liberation Front Partisans, once explained his understanding of the movement which could indicate the rationale for Jovanka's joining up. Adamic wrote that it was "a sudden promise of fulfillment of all the apparently futile and defeated political efforts on the part of the peasant or agrarian and other democratic parties of the previous people's government in Yugoslavia. LF was a way out to girls and young women who did not want to stay home and be raped by Germans or Italians, or sent to brothels behind the Russian front. It was better to go with their own men and help to kill the enemy, blow up trains and bridges and viaducts." *

The act of enlistment itself was not particularly significant to the young woman who had decided to cast her lot with the Partisans. It was only when she put on a uniform that the meaning of what she was doing came upon her—the fact that she was now a soldier and would have to kill suddenly seemed too difficult to face. Then she remembered what Serbian quislings had done—massacred fifty people of Pecane, friends she loved. From that time on she used a gun in memory of the victims of these traitors. Jovanka learned personally of the horror and tragedy of her adopted profession when she and three others became the only survivors of their unit after an attack on an Italian stronghold on the Dalmatian coast. And hardship was a constant companion which she shared with both men and women in the Partisan army. She often went barefoot in the snow and mud, existed on short rations, lived in cast-off clothing crawling with lice, was exposed to scurvy and trench mouth, spent many a bitter winter night on pine branches spread on the snow.

In an interview with the American writer Helen Worden

---

* Louis Adamic, *My Native Land*. Harper & Brothers, New York, 1943.

Erskine, Jovanka's stepmother stated that she did not know Jovanka with her short haircut and ill-fitting soldier's uniform hitched around the waist with a cartridge belt in which a pistol was stuck, when she came home from the front for the first time. Her grandmother said, "She was a warrior with a gun like anyone else." It was when Jovanka met another warrior with a gun, two years after her enlistment, that the wheel of fortune began to spin more favorably for the peasant girl. In time, the emaciated soldier would emerge as one of the most handsome, articulate, and best-dressed First Ladies of the world.

Jovanka was a private in the Partisan army when she was felled by typhus. Comrades carried her on a stretcher to the field hospital at the headquarters of Commander in Chief, Josip Broz Tito, who was now backed by Britain and the United States after they had supported for three years his Rightist rival, Mihajlovic. Tito, as a Marshal and head of the Army, had declared the royal government of Yugoslavia illegal.

Jovanka dismisses as fiction various stories about her first meeting with Tito. One of them held that at the time of her illness Stalin ignored Tito's request for antityphus serum thereby laying the groundwork for the eventual rupture of relations between the two governments. Another legend, according to Mme. Tito, was that she saved her future husband's life when he was caught in the midst of a battle and a German was aiming at him. She is supposed to have shot the Nazi. Jovanka's version of her first contact with her future husband was much less dramatic, as told to Mrs. Erskine:

> "I saw Tito first in 1944, as anybody would see him. I was merely one of the people." She said that her battalion had been assembled in the public square at Drarv to honor a young Partisan killed during the struggle in Bosnia. Tito made the funeral oration. Later, she shook hands with

him. "It was a great event for me," she recalled, "but I didn't know him really well until I went to work for him at the Secretariat in Belgrade. That was in 1945." *

When they met she was twenty and he was fifty-two.

Jovanka was a hospital administrator and political commissar with the rank of lieutenant when she joined Tito's Belgrade staff in 1945, but her job was really that of a filing clerk. She soon advanced to captain, and then to major, at which rank she was mustered out one year after her 1952 marriage to Tito. She has explained with a twinkle in her dark eyes that her husband ordered her demobilized since it seemed a little odd for the Marshal's wife to be a major.

The peasant girl who became the First Lady of Yugoslavia was born on December 7, 1924, in a Croatian village near the Bosnian border. At one time it seemed that she might become an American citizen. There was famine in the mountainous region of the Lika district where she lived in the late twenties and early thirties, and many of the local citizens decided that they might find life less difficult in the New World. Among those who migrated to the United States was her father Miko, a day laborer. He tried his unskilled hands at making a living in Chicago, San Francisco, and Cleveland, hoping to be able to earn enough money to send for Jovanka, her mother, sister, and two brothers. However, this was a period of depression in the United States, too. Miko decided to return home to his disappointed family in 1933. He spoke some English and was so full of intriguing stories about the distant land he had seen that the young Jovanka became interested in America and United States history.

A heavy burden was shifted to Jovanka's young shoulders at

* Helen Worden Erskine, *Collier's*, October 2, 1953.

the tender age of eleven. Her mother died in 1935 giving birth to the youngest daughter. The oldest left school at the fifth grade to take charge of the household and, in her own words, "shouldered a scythe, cut hay, cooked, baked, washed, ironed, housecleaned and sewed—just like any other peasant girl." *

Jovanka did not resume her education until after she was married, when she received her high school diploma and took entrance examinations for the university in Belgrade, where she majored in literature and art. She also set up her two sisters in an apartment in the capital because she wanted to give them the education she had been denied.

Her husband, Josip Broz, was born on May 25, 1892, in Kumrovec, Croatia, which was then part of the old Austro-Hungarian Empire. He was the seventh of fifteen children, eight of whom died when they were very young. At fifteen he became apprenticed to a locksmith and when he ran away was arrested for breaking his contract. Three years later he became a member of the Metal Workers Union and Social Democratic Party in Zagreb, capital of Croatia. He served in the Austro-Hungarian Army in World War I, and was wounded and captured by the Russians. During the year he was hospitalized—five hundred miles east of Moscow—he taught himself the language.

Tito—one of the pseudonyms he adopted during his conspiratorial career—joined the Bolshevik revolution in 1917. After two arrests by the White Russians and subsequent escapes, he was hidden by a seventeen-year-old Bolshevik girl—Pelagea (Polka) Byelusnova—who helped him flee to the Kirghiz mountains where he lived with nomads. He married Polka and took her to Yugoslavia in 1920, where their first baby died. Tito became an open member of the Communist Party and an agitator, which meant that he had to go underground when the party

* Helen Worden Erskine, *Collier's*, October 2, 1953.

was declared illegal. By 1925 he and Polka had three children, but only the boy Zarko survived. In 1928, while Tito was serving a long prison term for political activity, Polka returned to Russia with their son and later divorced her husband. She died in 1938. Tito married a Slovene—Berta Has—in 1938, and divorced her after World War II. She lived near the White Palace in Belgrade and worked for Radio Yugoslav. The son of this marriage and the two sons of Zarko, who is divorced and remarried, live with the President and Mme. Tito.

In 1941, after the Germans overran Yugoslavia, Tito organized the Leftist guerrillas, who were able to harass the occupation forces and give him the political footing on which to mount his leadership of Yugoslavia. He became a "loner" in the Communist world when the Cominform under the direction of the Soviet Union's Stalin began to denounce him in 1948 for various heresies. The USSR did not consider the Yugoslav party and governmental machinery reliable since it was created by Yugoslavs whose first loyalty was to Tito and not to agents of Moscow. By a complete commercial boycott in the summer of 1949, Stalin attempted to squeeze Tito into submission. Instead, the tough Yugoslav sought economic help from the United States and other Western nations, toward which he eased his own restrictions. After Stalin's death, the USSR began trying to woo Tito back into the Moscow-dominated camp. In June 1955 First Secretary Khrushchev and Premier Bulganin even visited Belgrade.

During this difficult period, Jovanka was very much at the Marshal's side. They were married but their wedding was kept a state secret for months. Mme. Broz was to disclose later, "We were married the twenty-fifth of April, 1952. The wedding was very private. I wore a red dress. We had a little party afterward at our home in Belgrade. My two younger sisters, Zora and Nada, came. That was all. We didn't announce it because here in Yugoslavia one's personal life is not a matter of public concern." * The marriage took place in Tito's mansion in Dedinje, a fashionable suburb of Belgrade. The town clerk officiated, since the Titos are not religious believers.

If Jovanka thought there was no public interest in the Marshal of Yugoslavia taking a new wife, she could not have been prepared for the wide publicity given the disclosure of the marriage nearly five months later. It was revealed through a simple invitation sent to members of the diplomatic corps bidding them to a reception for British Foreign Secretary and Mrs. Anthony Eden on September 19, 1952. The invitation read: "Marshal Josef Broz and Mrs. Josef Broz Tito cordially invite..."

The Associated Press on September 19, 1952, reported the occasion this way:

> A smiling, dark-eyed brunette of twenty-eight emerged as the first lady of Yugoslavia tonight. Eleven years ago she was a recruit in the Partisan Army.... In a chic burgundy evening gown, she made her first appearance in public as the third wife of the sixty-year-old Premier. The occasion was a reception in the ornate White Palace, seat of the government, in honor of British Foreign Secretary Eden. ... Mrs. Tito stole the show at the reception. Wives of the diplomatic corps, perhaps the most critical of all audiences, paid tribute to her charm and poise as she received guests on arrival and later circulated among them.... Tito was a proud bridegroom. She sat at his side during dinner while he chatted with Mr. Eden....

Someone at a reception once asked Jovanka why she had married Tito. She replied, "You may be disappointed. It had noth-

* Helen Worden Erskine, *Collier's,* October 2, 1953.

ing to do with socialism. I was—and am—in love with my husband."

During the secret months of their marriage, the couple had spent much of the time at the Marshal's favorite hideaway—the picturesque island of Brijoni. They had entertained Austrian Foreign Minister Gruber without the latter's suspecting his host and hostess were man and wife.

When Tito saw the impression Jovanka made at the Eden reception, he knew he had a valuable ally in his mate. He began to encourage her to appear at public functions, launch boats, and make world trips with him. She was at his side to receive chiefs of state and heads of government, including Prime Minister Nehru of India, Premier Guy Mollet of France, the Emperor of Ethiopia, and the King of Greece. At a lavish state party for Egypt's Prime Minister Nasser in a Belgrade palace resembling a miniature Versailles, the First Lady with her dark hair exquisitely coiffed and wearing a shimmering gown in the height of fashion, presided with stately grace. (Communist or not, Jovanka Tito dresses smartly—one of her designers is reported to be Klára Rothschild, described as the Communist oracle of fashion.) At this state function she took her husband and Nasser on a stroll through the former royal gardens and charmed them both with her presence and gay comment. When Khrushchev and Bulganin went to Yugoslavia in 1955 to try to patch up relations with Tito, they found the vivacious Jovanka always with her husband, not only for the festivities but for their business talks as well. Her presence on the latter occasions came as somewhat of a shock to the Soviet hierarchs accustomed as they were to operate conspiratorially. During this visit it is said that Khrushchev overindulged one evening in the native plum brandy and tried to kiss Jovanka. She took evasive action. Then the Russian suggested that they walk in the garden. This time an annoyed husband intervened. "It's past midnight," Tito snapped, "time to go to bed."

The sparkling First Lady of Yugoslavia began traveling abroad with her husband. She went with him to Paris, Cairo, Bucharest, and to the romantic island of Corfu, where they swam and relished the royal hospitality of Queen Frederika and King Paul. General Ne Win and his wife entertained them in Rangoon, Burma. When the Titos arrived in Rio, Jovanka was an immediate hit because she was wearing a yellow hat and green dress—the colors of Brazil. President Sukarno of Indonesia hosted an all-night New Year's Eve party for them on the exotic island of Bali, where the refreshments were supplemented by champagne and Yugoslavia's favorite beverage—slivovitz—brought ashore from the Marshal's yacht. Tito was slow to respond to Sukarno's urging that he swing with the Balinese dancing girls. However, as the party's tempo increased, Jovanka pulled her husband onto the floor. Soon the two Presidents in shirt sleeves and their wives were dancing the night away on the lawn.

When Jovanka first went with Tito to Moscow in 1959, she made a considerable contribution to the emancipation of Communist women. An American reporter wrote from the Soviet capital, "For the first time in the memory of most Soviet citizens, the wives of their collective comrades got a glimpse of the public and the public had a quickie look at the wives. It was a memorable occasion, but it was Jovanka who apparently convinced them that they should be seen. Naturally, she was seen with them." * She was pictured riding through Moscow in the back seat of the car with her husband while Khrushchev sat beside the driver.

In 1964, Mrs. Orville L. Freeman, wife of the United States

* New York *Post*, December 20, 1956.

Secretary of Agriculture, returned from a five-week tour of the Soviet Union and four other Communist countries and wrote:

"Marshal Tito's wife was the only one who had a real part of official life. She was the glamor girl of the whole bunch, a big hefty woman, but well proportioned, gorgeously dressed with pearls, diamond earrings and tremendous rings on both hands. Mrs. Broz was very chatty, even kidding Tito from time to time. And she obviously keeps up with everything." *

Jovanka taught the Communist men—including her husband —a thing or two, also. There was a notable example during the Khrushchev-Bulganin visit to Belgrade. The Titos were entertaining the Russians at a small, exclusive dinner party in the White Palace. Security men were keeping photographers at a considerable distance in an anteroom. An enterprising British cameraman, George Varjas, decided to go exploring. He went to the back of the building through the garden and there spotted Tito in his white uniform standing in front of a window. Just then a waiter opened it. Varjas pulled himself up to the sill—which was nine feet above the ground—and started taking pictures. What happened then, he described in *Look* magazine.

> . . . the whiz of the shutter was loud and clear when the conversation paused momentarily. Jovanka Broz turned and looked inquisitively at me from seven yards away. I was paralyzed. I looked at her lovely dark eyes and saw kindness and humor there. . . . I put my finger across my lips, begging her for silence. She burst out laughing.
>
> Tito's eyes followed his wife's; his expression darkened, but he said nothing. Bulganin, who at the moment seemed a kind old gentleman to me, saved the situation. "Photograph?" he exclaimed. Then, wagging his finger admonishingly, he told me, "Photographer, you will fall and break your neck." By this time, every person at the table was

* AP Feature, May 1964.

turning to see whom the old Soviet Premier was addressing.
A loud roar went up as they noticed me. . . .
. . . "Please do not give me away," I pleaded with them.
"I will be thrown out." Terrific laughter greeted this.

By this time, I was encouraged and I shouted in through
the window, "May I come in?" My friend, the beautiful
Jovanka, nodded yes. As I did so, I slipped, which brought
another roar of laughter. . . . Then, with Khrushchev wav-
ing his arm merrily at me and Bulganin still wagging his
finger, I ran out of film.

I asked to be excused as I had to fetch some more film.
. . . When I returned, it was Jovanka who heard me first
and she smiled at me. "Bravo," she cried, "it's the photographer again!" Gromyko, in English, yelled "Come in!"

The waiter came over to tell me that Mrs. Tito had
asked me to have a drink. I asked for champagne and got
it. Holding my glass high, I shouted in joy and triumph:
"Long live Jovanka, Tito, Khrushchev, Bulganin. . . ."
. . . I left as I came—through the window.

Around at the front of the palace again, I saw the guests
take their leave. As Jovanka told them good night, she
saw me. "Oh," she exclaimed with a mischievous smile,
"our window photographer." She held out the hand she
had just offered Bulganin. I kissed it too.*

The handsome Jovanka's style and wide-ranging interests
were evident when she accompanied her husband to Washington in October 1963. When Tito came down with the flu she
went off sight-seeing and shopping with Mrs. Angier Biddle
Duke, wife of the then United States Chief of Protocol. At the
National Gallery of Art she paused in appreciation before a
Rembrandt and remarked that there is "always something new
to see" in his pictures. She said they had some reproductions of
the painter's work in their Belgrade home. Looking at Goya's
"Bookseller," she commented, "He is the master."

* George Varjas, *Look*, July 12, 1955.

Jovanka accompanied her husband to the United Nations when he addressed the General Assembly. Then, like any tourist wishing to escape the big city, the President of Yugoslavia picked up a camera and took his wife to the country—to Sterling Forest some sixty miles from New York. Tito snapped pictures of a waterfall and they lunched at a cafeteria, carrying their own trays holding hamburgers and French fried potatoes.

At home, the First Lady of Yugoslavia has her choice of houses—the White Palace, a former archduke's *Schloss* in Slovenia, a villa on the island of Brijoni, and shooting lodges and rural hideaways all over the country. Once she chided Helen Worden Erskine for complimenting her on having so many lovely homes. "The houses are not mine," she said. "We only use them. They belong to the people."

Tito enjoys eating well, dressing well, and living in agreeable surroundings. He is happiest in the country shooting, riding, or swimming at his castle in Slovenia or at the villa on Brijoni, surrounded by children and his grandchildren, his friends and staff, various hangers-on who had been with him in the underground, dogs and horses. A permanent staff of housekeeper, butler, cook, and chauffeur accompany them to whichever house the First Family happens to be occupying at the moment, although each residence also has its own servants, gardeners, and caretakers.

Mme. Tito consults with the housekeeper each morning about the menus and other matters that require her attention. Then she visits one of her dressmakers, her tailor, milliner, or hairdresser. If there is time between state functions and her other activities, she may take a drive in the afternoon. And she does have other interests, such as maintaining contact with the various women's organizations of Yugoslavia. She has kept in close touch with the editorial boards of women's magazines. She is credited with inaugurating a discussion on toys, asking the designers to pay more attention to the psychological age of each group for which the toys are intended. The First Lady of Yugoslavia encourages her countrywomen by saying, "Before the revolutionary war women had no rights whatsoever. Today, a Yugoslav woman is limited only by her talents in entering any field of work."

Of course, Jovanka's first interest is always her husband—his health, welfare, and pleasure. Her extensive wardrobe is designed for his approval. She has said, "I choose colors that please Tito —white, green, red, black. He rarely comments on my clothes, but I know at once whether or not he approves. I had a flannel sport shirt I liked very much. The first time I wore it he said it was wrong for me. I rushed upstairs and took it off. Tito compromises, too. He even wears the gray sweater I knitted for him. Our tastes are similar. For example, we are both fond of pets. He has his dogs, canaries, pheasants, and fish. I've got two small bears at our Belgrade home." *

Politics remains one of the many common bonds between Jovanka and Tito. When asked if she was interested in this subject, she responded quickly, "Of course, I am interested in politics, and I follow actively what is happening in the world and in the country and very often I discuss these events with my husband, but I do not take an active part in it myself." To the inquiry of another interviewer, Mrs. Erskine, as to whether she ever discusses politics with her husband, her reply was, "Of course —local and international. Why shouldn't I? I took part in the struggle, too. But I never attempt to interfere in his business or to influence him. You might say I am his sounding board." *

* Helen Worden Erskine, *Collier's*, October 2, 1953.

Tahia Nasser

7.

Tahia Nasser—United Arab Republic

O N a hot Cairo night in July 1952 a swarthy, handsome Egyptian officer climbed the three flights of steps to his four-room apartment on plain, tree-shaded Galal Street near the military base of Abbassia. It was well after midnight when he tiptoed into the bedroom where he was sure his wife was asleep. However, Tahia Nasser, with that sixth sense she had developed from living for eight years with a man whose coming and going had become increasingly mysterious, knew her husband was home again. Through half-opened eyes, she saw him shove a crate under the bed. "Oranges again," she thought, "probably from Hakim." Pleased by the windfall and secure in the knowledge that once more Gamal had returned safely, the dark-haired young woman drifted off into untroubled slumber.

Shortly after dawn Tahia slipped quietly out of bed so as not to disturb her sleeping mate. Remembering the oranges, she decided to have fresh juice for breakfast. She stooped down to pull out the box but it would not budge. So she put in her hand to get some of the fruit. Suddenly Tahia Nasser was looking at a hand grenade!

Stifling an impulse to cry out, she carefully and fearfully returned the lethal object to the crate and crept out of the room. She had not uttered a sound, for she had grown accustomed to the unexpected in her existence. Later, when her six-foot-two spouse flashed his gleaming smile at the kitchen door to let her know he was up and about, there was no mention of oranges—or hand grenades—in her cheerful greeting. She had known when she married that it would be useless to expect any real confidences from a man who lived by Nasser's code. He had said, "I'm suspicious of everyone. I cannot help it. I cannot open my heart to anyone." Nevertheless, a slight innuendo of woman's curiosity crept into her solicitous inquiry, "You must be very tired from all your work of planning—whatever you are planning."

Her husband chose to ignore the opportunity for confession. Instead, he bounced his 2½-year-old son Khaled in the air, inquired after their daughters, Hoda and Mona, who were already at play with the neighborhood children, and sat down to breakfast.

When the Lieutenant-Colonel left for his duties at the Army Staff College, Tahia could not help thinking about the recent growing pace of unexplained events. There had been mysterious telephone messages she was asked to relay to him, strangers who showed up at the apartment, his frequent absences until far into the night, and closed-door meetings with other officers around the golden oak table at which he had just eaten his breakfast. Then there had been that annoying interruption of their vacation in Alexandria earlier in the month. Gamal had received a message ordering him to return to Cairo immediately —and the reason seemed so trivial. He was needed to grade examination papers at the staff college!

Tahia's long-held suspicion that her husband was engaged in some type of political intrigue was confirmed by an incident a few days before they went on holiday. They both were exceedingly fond of motion pictures and tried to go to the cinema once or twice a week. However, that routine was suffering because of Gamal's late hours. This particular evening he had suggested a movie. Eagerly she rushed dinner and hustled the children to bed and they were soon off in their little Austin. As they drove through the Cairo suburb at dusk, Nasser suddenly slowed down, drew over to the curb, and pulled on the brake. He said he remembered that he had to see an officer who lived in the house before which they had stopped. He promised not to be gone long.

Tahia settled down to wait. A half hour passed—and then an hour. Feeling a little cramped, she decided to adjust the seat so as to be able to stretch her legs. As she pushed back the seat, a pile of pamphlets that had been stuffed underneath came into view. Tahia picked up one and looked at it. She read a leaflet printed by the secret Free Officers Committee. It condemned King Farouk and the presence of British troops in Egypt and demanded that both be ousted.

Here was incriminating evidence in their own car that her husband was involved in rebellion! Like most Army wives in Cairo, she was aware the Committee existed, but knew little about it. What she did not know was that Gamal was the founder and leader of the Free Officers Committee, about which he had sworn all members to the strictest secrecy. The organization had grown out of resentment over British influence in the country.

This had been fanned into an independence movement when Farouk in 1942 yielded to a show of force by the British at the Palace and appointed a pro-Allied Prime Minister instead of the Nazi supporter he had originally selected. A number of young officers, headed by Nasser, were infuriated over this British pressure and the King's weakness. They later added to their grievances the corruption and inefficiency in the military high command that contributed to the humiliating defeat by Israel in 1948.

Realizing the gravity of the evidence she had come upon, Tahia quickly restored the seat to its original position. When her husband returned—much too late to go to the movies—the pamphlets were out of sight and she pretended to be napping.

Some years later Tahia Nasser could read in her husband's own words what his secret life was like at that time. He recorded in his autobiography: "Our life during that period was like an exciting detective story. We had dark secrets and passwords; we used to lurk in the shadows; we used to collect pistols and hand grenades and the firing of bullets was the hope we dreamed about. We made many attempts in this direction."

Not long after the grenade incident Tahia learned more—but not all—about Gamal's involvement in the underground movement. On the night of July 20, 1952, he and six other officers held one of their secret meetings around the golden oak table on Galal Street. Two mornings later, Nasser remained in bed so late that his daughters asked their mother if he was ill. Finally he arose, apparently in the best of health, ate a large combination breakfast and lunch, and set out for the Staff College. He returned to the apartment late that night, bathed and changed into a fresh uniform. The children were asleep, and he told Tahia not to wait up, as he was assigned to special duty. Two strangers arrived with a message. Nasser's brothers Leithy and

Shawky, who were schoolteachers, were listening to the radio. He beckoned them to follow him into the hall. There he whispered, "I've got two hundred Egyptian pounds here. I am going to save one pound for myself and give you the rest. If anything happens to me tonight, give the money to Tahia. With this, added to the income from her inheritance, she'll be all right. But you must promise to keep an eye on her and the children." The brothers gave their word—and Nasser was gone to carry out the operation he had set in motion two nights earlier. This is the way he tells it:

> On July 20 I called a meeting of seven Free Officers who formed the hard core of the Revolution Command and informed them that I had decided to act . . . ninety officers with small arms only, were all that were available to take over a nation.
> I drew up the basic plan after that meeting in my house and gave it to Abdel Hakim Amer to work out the details. I put off the deadline to 1 A.M. July 23. At about 10 P.M. on July 22 an Intelligence Officer and one of our members came around to my house in Cairo with a warning that King Farouk had contacted the Chief of General Staff and called a conference for eleven o'clock to take action against us. Amer and I set out to collect some troops from the Abbassia barracks.*

During the night of July 22-23, Tahia was awakened by gunfire. Her immediate thought was for her husband. She called his brothers and asked if they knew where Gamal was. They told her about the money and instructions. Anxiously she switched on the radio. At last there was a news bulletin. Radio Cairo announced that the Free Officers were in control of the city.

Shortly afterward the doorbell rang. There stood a personal

* Gamal Abdel Nasser, *The Philosophy of the Revolution*. Economica Books, Smith, Keynes and Marshall, Buffalo, N.Y., 1959.

emissary from Gamal, an old friend, Sarwat Okasha, with a message for Tahia. During a press conference on the coup held by Maj. Gen. Mohammed Naguib (later to be revealed as a front for Nasser), Gamal had called Sarwat aside and whispered, "Go to my home and tell Tahia what's happened. I don't want her to worry. But tell her I made a promise to myself not to return home until Farouk is out of the country. I don't know when that will be."

When Sarwat went back to Nasser to report that his mission had been accomplished, he remarked, "I think she knew what we had been up to all along."

Tahia had to wait three more days before seeing her husband. On July 26, gross, dissolute Farouk boarded the yacht *Mahroussa* at Alexandria and sailed into ignominious exile—a king without a throne, a man without a country. Nasser had forced him to abdicate.

The coup brought a change in the life of Tahia and the children, although she still did not know that her husband was the real power in Egypt. She followed his instructions to prepare to move from their apartment to a modest five-room bungalow formerly occupied by an Army schoolmaster just beyond the Abbassia barracks on the outskirts of the city. Nasser had ordered the key members of the new regime, most of whom—except Naguib—belonged to the Free Officers Committee, to locate in the military compound of Manchiat el Bakry.

Tahia liked the new house. The high walls around the compound ensured protection and privacy for her family, and the nearby homes of other officials provided neighbors and friends for herself and the children. At this time there were daughters Hoda and Mona, who had been born in 1946 and 1947, and sons Khaled and Abdel-Hamik, born in 1949 and 1951. Hakim Amer arrived in 1953. After the birth of the second daughter

Tahia, mindful of the Muslim concern for male heirs, had remarked to Gamal, "Next time we'll have a boy." She had more than fulfilled the promise with three sons!

As Tahia busied herself with the growing family, her husband worked sixteen- to twenty-hour days in reforming the governing machinery. At first he authorized the creation of a regency to rule until Farouk's young son should come of age. However, in June 1953 he decided to abolish the monarchy altogether and declare Egypt a republic. Naguib continued as Prime Minister, but Nasser began to emerge from the shadows by taking over the portfolios of Deputy Prime Minister and Minister of the Interior. Finally, in 1954, Nasser maneuvered Naguib out of office and assumed the number-one spot officially. He became President in 1956.

There was no serious discussion in the family about moving into any one of the many royal palaces that had been the scenes of such riotous living in the days of the monarchy. The new ruler was determined to belittle and brand with disrepute anything connected with the Farouk reign. Newspaper and magazine exposés were directed to emphasize the excesses of the former King and his cronies. Every lurid detail of their extravagances and escapades was recited and embellished in the Egyptian press. At the same time, Nasser insisted that puritanism and simplicity were to govern the behavior of members of his official family. They were not to be seen at the gambling casinos or racetracks, or in the notorious nightclubs and expensive restaurants that had enjoyed royal patronage. Nasser also had a concept of family life that did not fit into palace surroundings. "In the palaces, each of us would be living in his own apartment. We would be a divided family. Out here, in our house, we all live together."

"Besides," he added, laughing at the recollection, "we moved to Tahira Palace for a few weeks while they were building the new wing in our house. The children began playing in the corridors and started breaking priceless vases and art treasures. I have to pay for everything they break. I cannot afford to live in a palace."

It had become necessary to expand the five-room cottage to accommodate the enlarging family and the increasing functions of the head of the government. The tiny foyer off a bedroom was scarcely adequate as a study and reception room for conferences of state. Beyond the gate, which is guarded day and night, there are now a tennis court and library. The front of the house is banked with hundreds of flowering plants. At the rear there is a swimming pool and an extensive lawn edged with trees. Inside the house there is a large *salon* with a marble fireplace, a crystal chandelier, Louis XIV furniture, oriental and prayer rugs where the Chief of State receives guests. Mme. Nasser has her own smaller drawing room to entertain friends. It contains a piano on which she plays with modest talent the works of Chopin, Rachmaninoff, and other classical composers. Sometimes she has even been induced to give private concerts. She is an expert at needlepoint. There is a small theater where the Nassers can indulge their continuing enjoyment of motion pictures without going into Cairo.

All in all, however, the official residence looks more like the home of a well-to-do executive than the mansion of a powerful ruler. The lack of pretension is a carry-over from Nasser's childhood experience and is easily shared by the retiring young woman who fell in love with a bitter, lonely officer nearly a quarter of a century before. For Tahia Nasser's first concern throughout her marriage has been to be a good wife, mother, and housekeeper. She has shown little taste for the pomp and position of a public figure, and would be unlikely to do so even if her husband were to reverse his view that her place is in their home.

When Nasser came to power, Tahia quickly established a smooth-running household that accommodated the very different needs of her husband and the children. Gamal is always the first to arise—between six and seven. He breakfasts alone on tea, white cheese, a bowl of bread and milk, and a dish of *foul*—a native bean concoction—and then goes to his office, which is in another building on the grounds. Tahia has breakfast with the children when they are home. Before school age, she gave them their first lessons in Arabic, English, and French. She is a good linguist and had attended a French preparatory school in Cairo. As they grew older she saw her children off to school.

The private time for husband and wife is at lunch. They have this meal together, and telephone interruptions are forbidden unless there is an emergency. Afterward, the President reads the afternoon papers and takes a siesta during the heat of the day. At five o'clock he returns to work for eight or nine hours longer unless there is an official function to attend. Tahia dines with the children—and sometimes with friends—at eight.

As in the days of the conspiracy, many official conferences are held far into the night, either in Nasser's study or the *salon*. The late Dag Hammarskjöld told of talking into the early morning hours with the Egyptian leader at the time of the Suez crisis. At midnight, Tahia has a tray of food sent to her husband. Coffee, juice, and cigarettes are constantly replenished by a servant. Nasser does not drink liquor, but he consumes some twenty cups of syrupy black Turkish coffee and smokes three packages of American cigarettes a day. In her quiet, devoted way, Tahia has created the home where this intense, complex man can find the relaxation which makes it possible for him to carry out his arduous duties. Gamal had selected his wife not for her beauty but because she appeared to possess the qualities that ensured a steadfast marriage partner and capable mother. She has fully demonstrated these talents, even serving as a kind of father to their offspring when Nasser's preoccupation with affairs of state has kept him from the hearthside.

Nasser, the son of a postal clerk, was born on January 15, 1918, in a modest suburb of Alexandria notable for its heat, dust, and mud huts. The area was surrounded by villas of rich French landowners from whom emanated the social snobbery of the privileged classes. This naturally aroused deep hostility in the young Gamal. Shortly after coming to power years later, Nasser decreed that no Egyption could own more than two hundred acres of land.

A tragedy in Gamal's early life also conditioned the man who was to be: the death of his mother. He was the oldest of four children and his mother's favorite. When he was eight she insisted that he go to Cairo to attend a good school. It was not until Gamal returned at the end of the first term that he learned why his mother had not answered his daily letters. She had died in childbirth. The uncle with whom he had lived in the capital said this tragic loss colored the boy's outlook and led to his being called "the somber cadet" when he was in military school. This painful separation from one he loved when so young probably influenced Nasser to stay away from palaces after taking over the government because, "Out here in our house we all live together." In the dark-eyed Tahia he had found the woman who was to fill the emptiness in his life and give him the family he wanted to keep together. However, he had some difficulty obtaining her hand.

Tahia Mahmoud Kazem was born in Cairo in 1923. Her grandfather had come from Persia. Her father was a prosperous merchant of Persian imports, particularly tea. She had two sisters and a brother. When her parents died and her older sister married, Tahia went to live with her only brother, Abdel-Hamid Kazem, who owned a small rug factory near the Abbassia military academy where Gamal Abdel Nasser was an instructor. The two men were friends, and Nasser frequently visited the Kazem home. There he was attracted to the warm kindliness of the younger sister, noting her skill in housekeeping. Finally, Gamal approached Abdel-Hamid with a proposal of marriage for the young lady. But the brother brushed him off. After all, the suitor at the time did not appear to have promising financial or career prospects. The small landholding of the Nassers would have to be divided among so many that little would be left for Gamal. By contrast, Tahia had inherited securities that gave her some two hundred dollars a month—a small fortune in a country where the average yearly income was a hundred dollars. Moreover, the lieutenant had in his record a notation by superior officers that he was "insubordinate, an independent troublemaker." Besides all this, Abdel-Hamid was perhaps not enthusiastic about losing such a good housekeeper.

However, Gamal would not be put off. Kazem finally told his sister that Nasser wanted to marry her, and to his great surprise she said she would like to accept. On the first day of Gamal's furlough in 1944 they signed a Muslim marriage contract in the presence of a few close friends—mostly from the Army. She was twenty-one. He was twenty-five.

Tahia had reason to suspect that she was marrying a man whose interest extended beyond the military to politics. For one thing, a scar on his forehead just under the hairline was visible evidence of his part in an anti-British demonstration in 1935. He had been clubbed and jailed for participation in a student riot, and she knew he had been arrested several times for youth-ful revolutionary activities.

Any woman who becomes the wife of a soldier must accept the fact that there will be continual anxiety in her life. In 1948 Major Nasser was reported killed in action at Irak-El-Manshia in the war with Israel. However, he had only been wounded and was soon back at the front.

A year later Tahia realized more clearly that her husband's career, and even his life, could be endangered by political ac-tivity. One evening she went to the Cairo station to meet him on his return for a furlough with his family. She saw the military police pick him up, instead. Later she learned that he had been taken to the headquarters of the Chief of Staff who, in turn, had escorted him to the Prime Minister and Military Gov-ernor of Egypt. There he was accused of plotting against the government. However, Nasser answered the challenge and was cleared.

After the successful coup in 1952, Tahia's anxiety lessened. Surely now her husband was safe from harm. In less than two years, however, she was to learn that the wife of a leader in the volatile Middle East can never rest easily about her husband's safety. In 1954, as Nasser was speaking in Alexandria, eight shots were fired at him. Tahia kept a lone and anxious vigil beside the radio for details, to hear at last that the bullets had missed their mark. Her husband had merely paused long enough in his speech to shout, "Be calm. Don't be afraid. We are all masters." Nevertheless, the attack stabbed a new fear into her heart that has never completely subsided. Nearly every year there has been some new threat of assassination.

When Gamal Abdel Nasser assumed the position of Egypt's Chief of State, his wife became First Lady, by Western stand-ards. However, the President had a very different idea about the role of his mate. In part because of his effort to restore Egypt's dignity after all of Farouk's philandering, Nasser suggested that official ladies should appear in public as little as possible, and then under the most discreet circumstances. Tahia was quite content to follow this idea, glad that it meant no disruption of her modest way of living. In the early years of his presidency, Nasser acted as host at state functions in the palaces, but always alone. He accepted invitations only for himself even when the wives of other officials were on the guest list.

By 1959 Tahia had attended only two state dinners and these were farewell functions for retiring British and American ambassadors. In that year, she and the children accompanied her husband on a formal visit to Yugoslavia—the family's first trip away from Egypt. She was photographed with Marshal Tito and his wife, and the two women became fast friends. Although pictures of the visit appeared in foreign newspapers, they were not printed in the Egyptian press. The following year, Tahia was in a group picture with Emperor Haile Selassie during the Ethiopian ruler's visit to Egypt, but the caption did not identify her. Whether because of Tahia's desire for privacy, or Nasser's insistence upon it, his wife usually remained out of pictures until the Nikita Khrushchevs came to call in 1964.

If Tahia Nasser has missed the glamour and duties customarily associated with First Ladies, she has had other compensations. She has enjoyed a freedom permitted few of her rank. She can shop unrecognized and, therefore, without security guards. With a woman companion she visits the Cairo stores to buy her grandchildren's clothing that she does not make herself, and to purchase her own simple Western garments. When her daughters became teen-agers their mother allowed them the privilege of making their own selections for their wardrobes in the Cairo shops.

She attends concerts, opera, and the ballet as just one of many women, and stops at a café afterward, if she chooses, for coffee and pastry. More than once she has heard her husband speak from a place as inconspicuous as that in Alexandria in 1956 when she listened to him deliver one of his most important addresses. Before a hundred thousand people massed in Liberation Square she heard Nasser proclaim, "Suez belongs to us." She was sitting, not on the platform beside the President, but in an obscure seat on the balcony of a nearby building.

However, life is changing for Tahia Nasser. Her daughter Hoda married the son of a former deputy minister at their suburban Cairo residence in the summer of 1965, with President Sekou Touré of Guinea among the thousand guests. The second daughter, Mona, was married in the fall of the same year to a first lieutenant in the Army. Khaled and Abdel-Hamid are in secondary school, where young Hakim will soon be joining them.

As the children are growing up and leaving home, Tahia, still young and energetic in her forties, finds more time to spend on her music and needlepoint. She maintains her long-time custom of entertaining at a relaxing dinner once a month their oldest and closest friends, some of whom have lowly stations in life. This gives Gamal an opportunity to hear views outside government circles.

In some ways the house is the same, and in others it is different. There are many memories—like the time when a little boy on a tricycle scooted through the room in which her husband was having an important conference with the American Ambassador. And one day the President of Egypt apologized good-naturedly to an interviewer for the glasses and plates stacked on the table of a reception room because there were sudden guests for dinner that night, and Tahia had borrowed extra tableware. No longer can a visitor hear a Nasser youngster bawling his objections as Tahia tries to put him to bed. However, grandchildren are bringing back the childish sounds.

Naturally, there is still an atmosphere of eternal vigilance around the residence as guards pace the grounds. And noisy teletypes, telephones, and radios keep the Chief of State in constant touch with his country and the troubled world. Suez is Egyptian, but the United Arab Republic continues to face grave problems with Israel, in Yemen, and elsewhere in the Middle East. Tahia Nasser seems happy because she is close to the man she married. To strangers she refers to him as *El Raís*, meaning the President. To friends she shifts slightly the accent and inflection to give the colloquialism for "The Boss, *El Rayis*." He will always be that to her. And no doubt that is all she ever really wants—except for freedom from anxiety for her husband's life which haunts any wife of a leader in that part of the world.

8.

Fathia Nkrumah—Ghana

YOUNG Egyptian woman with the creamy olive skin, dark eyes and hair of an Elizabeth Taylor—to echo an observer—arrived secretly in Accra, capital of Ghana, in December 1957. She was escorted by a doctor-uncle and a minister of the government. Tucked in her luggage was lingerie purchased in the best shops of Cairo with money from her dowry. For her this amounted to three hundred Egyptian pounds. She also carried gifts from Egypt's President Nasser—former royal jewels and the Grand Cordon of the Order of the Nile.

Fathia Halim Ritzk had come to marry a forty-eight-year-old man she had never met before. The waiting groom had been the first Negro Prime Minister of a British colony. Kwame Nkrumah now ruled newly independent Ghana, which nestled under the western hump of Africa in a region once called the Gold Coast.

Within a few hours after the arrival of his bride-to-be, Nkrumah summoned four cabinet ministers and his mother to an-

Fathia Nkrumah

cient Christianborg Castle, the white citadel with its crenellated battlements that was built overlooking the Gulf of Guinea by Danish slavers in the seventeenth century. There, in a private civil ceremony, the daughter of the Nile who spoke no English became the wife of the English-speaking African who did not understand Arabic. But it was hoped this marriage of convenience would fulfill the prophecy of Nkrumah's soothsayer.

A few months earlier the "holy one" had told his exalted follower, "Africa's messiah will be the son of an African man and an Egyptian woman." The prediction had greatly impressed Nkrumah, who had never surrendered his belief in African magic, incantations and readings of the future, although as a boy he was baptized a Roman Catholic and was schooled in missions of the faith in Assima and Sekondi. The soothsayer had seen the vision of a dynasty, which confirmed the aspirations of a man who already harbored messianic ambitions of his own.

There was only one drawback to Nkrumah's instant desire to try to help shape his manifest destiny. He had always said he never wanted to become entangled with a woman because of his admitted fear of the female of the species from his earliest days, a fear which he confessed was "beyond all understanding." His attitude may have had some relevance to the close association with his "mammy trader" mother, who sold cigarettes and rice while his father worked as a goldsmith. He insisted on sleeping in his mother's bed. Nkrumah once said, "I used to be angry when my father came to sleep in our bed. . . . I told him that I was also married to her and it was my job to protect her."

But to many it appeared that Nkrumah's real fear was for the entanglement of matrimony rather than of women. At the time of his marriage he already had a teen-age son. (This son was serving his medical residency at Children's Hospital Medical Center in Boston in 1966.)

However, any momentary hesitation Nkrumah had about accepting wedlock was dispelled by the tantalizing thought that he might sire Africa's messiah. He soon moved to assist the good spirits beckoning him toward a high place in history. He called in a Muslim friend from Upper Volta, Sinare, who was teaching Arabic in Accra, and commissioned him to go to Egypt and find the woman who could fulfill the words of the prophet.

"What I need is a wife like yours," Nkrumah said. But he actually preferred a Christian, someone who shared his religious belief.

The search for the bride was undertaken in general secrecy but with the knowledge of President Nasser. It soon narrowed down to five Coptic families, inasmuch as the Copts represented the most ancient and purest Egyptian stock and were, therefore, of the lineage from which a leader might come.

The home in which the mission reached a successful conclusion was a modest one in the Cairo suburb of Zeitun. Here lived the widow of a clerk in the Egyptian telephone company and her five children. The oldest was Fathia.

The young lady had received most of her education from the Sisters of Our Lady of the Apostles, who had taught her some French. She had also studied Arabic at the University of Cairo. She displayed no particular talent or any special interest in anything beyond the narrow range of activity permitted by the limited means of her family.

At twenty-six, Fathia was somewhat advanced in years for a marriage prospect—especially by Egyptian standards. A younger sister seemed better qualified in this respect. But Mrs. Ritzk held out for her firstborn. Although Fathia had the Taylor coloring, she was not pretty. Her features were broader and more

Slavlike than those of the actress. It was generally conceded she was handsome. Her figure was inclined toward plumpness except for the slim waistline, in which her future husband was to take pride.

Nkrumah's courier spread pictures of the prospective bride-groom before the Ritzk family for their inspection. When he received a photograph of Fathia, he rushed back to Accra for approval of his mission. He also carried likenesses of several young Muslim women. Nkrumah is reported to have been impressed by two of the latter, but remembering the factor of religion, he decided on Coptic Fathia. He declared they were engaged but ordered that this news be kept from both the Ghanaian and the Egyptian people. And although rumors spread in Accra that the leader was about to take a wife, there was no official confirmation until the government radio made the announcement the night of the wedding.

There was some reason for withholding as long as possible the news of the union of the popular Negro bachelor and a white woman of another country. All unbetrothed Ghanaian women could dream of being chosen as long as Nkrumah remained eligible—which was not an inconsiderable element in maintaining his popularity level. Moreover, the selection of a white woman risked an outburst of resentment among those who believed that only a Negro was worthy of the Prime Minister of Ghana.

Mme. Nkrumah was soon to learn how Ghanaian women felt about her. Not long after their marriage, as Nkrumah was unveiling a statue of himself, Fathia moved close to him. Angry African women broke through the police cordon and swept her aside.

It was soon apparent that Fathia Ritzk was not prepared—by training, experience, or temperament—for the role which the

African mystic had ordained for her. Unable to speak the language, strange to the ways of West Africa and the culture of the country, and alone among the people of a foreign race, Fathia, who was already shy by nature, gave the impression of being a "simple, sullen woman."

She was married to a total stranger with whom she could not communicate until, following his instructions, she began taking lessons in English. She was to learn of the loneliness of marriage to a man who had said that if he "allowed a woman to play too important a part in my life I would gradually lose sight of my goal." Some measure of that goal was implicit in the titles he had assumed: The Redeemer, *Osagyefo* (Great Man), *Katamanto* (Man Whose Word Is Irrevocable), *Nufenu* (Strongest of All). He had a Western education—holding B.A. and Bachelor of Sacred Theology degrees from Lincoln University, Oxford, Pennsylvania, and an M.A. in anthropology from the University of Pennsylvania—but he was frequently guided by African superstitions. He carried a cane to ward off evil, and for the same reason little leather bags were attached to his chair after complicated ministrations, the pouring of libations and the occasional sacrifice of a sheep by a jujuman.

Fathia was also not prepared to assume direction of the official household. Her Pygmalion requested the British wife of Dr. H. Kamuzu Banda—Prime Minister of Malawi—to take over that responsibility until his Galatea learned the routine. Among several American Negro women enlisted to instruct the Egyptian pupil in her role was a doctor who taught Fathia chess and occasionally prepared an American dish for her to sample.

Nkrumah instilled in Fathia a preoccupation with maintaining a slim figure. A Ghanaian who was asked what people in Accra talked about most in discussing the First Lady, replied that it was whether she was gaining or losing weight. In conversation she was described as sweet but without displaying any particular intellectual interest or taste. She wore the native shapeless Kenti cloth dress with no notable distinction. Her Western gowns displayed an extra flounce, ribbon, or furbelow with a pinched-in waist that exaggerated her weight, particularly at the hips. She wore her hair in a high teased fashion regardless of the current style. Over the coiffure she placed a deep-crowned cloche whenever a hat was called for.

During the first year of the marriage, a friend recalls several incidents as proof of the affection between the Nkrumahs. When a film of one of their public appearances was shown, *Osagyefo* patted his wife's hand and said, "You're photogenic." She smiled her thanks. When Fathia was listening to her husband on the radio, one of his followers said, "He is wonderful." She responded, "You speak true." When a longtime Nkrumah acquaintance remarked that she was so glad he was happy, the Prime Minister replied, "I'm happier than most people would imagine. Fathia is a wonderful, pure, sweet girl, and I am deeply in love with her. I thought a wife would hinder me, but no. She is completely self-effacing and not demanding. Everybody around me is completely dedicated. They have to be." This may have sounded to another woman like romantic surrender of previously held narrow concepts of marriage. But in fact it was the natural response of a self-centered revolutionary still determined that no woman—or man, for that matter— could make him lose sight of his goal.

When the first child—a boy—arrived in 1959, the father, of course, was very proud. The name Gamal was bestowed on the prospective messiah, after the President of Egypt. Daughter Samia came in 1960. But when the youngest son, Sekou, named for the President of Guinea, was born in 1963, such mystery surrounded the occasion that there is still speculation as to whether the infant was abnormal in some way, or if he even survived.

Fathia's lack of experience in coping with the role suddenly thrust upon her in a foreign capital, understandably kindled frustration and a kind of rebellion in the woman who seemed to her husband so self-effacing. Resentment was fed by anxiety over the repeated attempts to assassinate Nkrumah. There is no record of Fathia offering him counsel, but a Ghanaian asserts that during one period of personal and political tension she warned her husband that he was accepting bad advice from some of his associates. As threats mounted, the naturally suspicious leader began retreating more and more into a self-imposed isolation, knowing that many former friends had turned against him for one reason or another and fearful that others were plotting to do the same. The Nkrumahs moved from Christianborg Castle to the impregnable Flagstaff House located in the midst of two hundred heavily fortified acres in the heart of Accra.

The impact of the various pressures produced in the First Lady what one resident called "fits." There came the day in 1962 when she packed her bags and left for the airport, determined to return to her home in Egypt. Nkrumah retreated briefly from his lofty refusal to allow a woman to make him lose sight of his goal. He went to the airport and brought her back. Reports of other similar incidents have not been confirmed. But the previous year she had gone to Cairo and received the official welcome of the highest dignitaries of her native land. The announced purpose of the visit was to inaugurate an airline between the two countries. However, she stayed for two months—without her husband.

When a Ghanaian who was familiar with the 1962 episode was asked whether "other women" were involved, he laughed and said, "there have always been and always will be women" in the life of Nkrumah. In fact, the aspiring Messiah had written in his autobiography in 1957, "However unconventional and un-satisfactory ... [polygamy] may appear to those who are con-firmed monogamists, and without in any way trying to defend my own sex, it is a frequently accepted fact that man is naturally polygamous."

Whatever the reason, the lonely woman from Cairo who had no personal social life, outside of entertaining a few friends in the seclusion of her home, began appearing at public functions with increasing frequency. She carried the title of Chief Patron of the National Council of Ghana Women and Honorary Chief of Ghana Girl Guides, showing herself at ceremonial occasions for these organizations as well as when her husband presented honors to members of the National Gliding School. In June 1965 Mme. Nkrumah was at the Accra airport with her two older children to participate in what was called a "hero's wel-come" when Kwame Nkrumah returned from the Common-wealth Prime Ministers Conference in London. In July of that year she appeared with the nation's leader when he inaugurated Ghana television, and the following month when he opened parliament with pomp and circumstance.

The most extensive official responsibility Mme. Nkrumah undertook was in March 1965, when Ghana's First Lady paid a two-day visit to Ho, administrative headquarters of the Volta Region. A grand durbar of chiefs was held in her honor. She distributed certificates to women who had attended a child-care course organized by the Ministry of Social Welfare. She laid the foundation stone of a health clinic, which was to pro-vide a forum for classes where mothers would be able to learn about child welfare and prenatal care. She was made an Hon-orary Queen Mother and was presented with many gifts. Mme.

Nkrumah made a speech in which she said: "As mothers, the health of our children is our first responsibility, for these little ones are the future of our country."

The First Lady of Ghana had at last found a common bond with the women of another race and land with whom she had taken up her abode. However, the man who ruled her life as well as theirs still made sure that she would remain self-effacing, dedicated only to him. To a request for information about her, an aide replied: "I regret to inform you that *Osagyefo* does not feel favorably inclined to Madame's participation in the projected book." Perhaps the Redeemer had a premonition there would be a delay in fulfillment of the prophecy that his seed would lead Africa to the promised land. On February 24, 1966, while Nkrumah and a large official party (some as hostages) were in Peking, the Ghana armed forces and police took over the government. The rule of the Great Man had come to an end abruptly and ignominiously. He made his way to Guinea to await the advice of his soothsayers.

Fathia Nkrumah took her children and returned home to Egypt, confident that this time she would not be forced to return to Ghana.

9.

Daw Thein Tin
(Mme. Thant)—
United Nations

*T*HE dark-eyed bride wore the holy color of
Burma on her wedding day—a native *longyi* in yellow. With
the long skirt were a white blouse and stole. Sandals of velvet,
once the footgear of royalty, were on her feet. Her jewels were a
diamond choker, bracelet and comb set in a high pile of black
hair. The groom followed the bride's choice of color for his
longyi and observed a custom he usually preferred to ignore by
donning a yellow *baung-baung,* or cloth turban with a floating
end at one side found in the traditional wardrobe of a Burmese
man.

Saturday-born Ma Thein Tin and Friday-born Maung Thant
had selected this November day in 1934 for their wedding only
after consulting the astrologers about an appropriate date.
Burmese rarely make an important decision without seeking the
advice of the stargazers. In preparation for this life-long practice,

Daw Thein Tin with her husband, U Thant,
and her daughter, Aye Aye

the birth of a child is clocked to the second so that his horoscope can be cast exactly.

The scene of the nuptials was the richly appointed home of Ma Thein Tin's widowed mother and grandparents in Pantanaw, a small town in lower Burma surrounded by miles of rice fields and fish ponds. There were no saffron-robed Buddhist monks present, since a Burmese marriage is a civil rite. The ceremony was the usual one. First, the couple sat side by side and listened while a townsman recited a panegyric he had composed about them, their parents and grandparents, after which he gave them *thabye* (eugenia) leaves. They made deep obeisance before the statue of Lord Buddha and put the leaves into a silver bowl, going through the same performance six times in order to honor the Way, the monkhood, their parents, teachers, elders, and guests. Then a happily married older couple put their hands together and into the bowl while the eulogist said three times, *"Aung Bye,"* or "It is successful." They were now man and wife to be showered with confetti, colored rice, and new coins. The guests looked at the wedding gifts, inspected the bridal chamber where the women wanted to be sure the blankets were of velvet, as tradition demanded, feasted and toasted the bride and groom in nonalcoholic beverages. The newlyweds remained in Ma Thein Tin's home for their honeymoon as was the custom.

The bride observed Burmese fashion by not taking her husband's name. However, as years and position were added, it was natural for her to become known as Daw Thein Tin rather than Ma Thein Tin. Thant had been given only that name by his family. However, Maung, which is the designation of youth, is still retained in Thant's signature as a mark of humility. Long ago he was entitled to the venerable title of "U," which literally means "uncle."

Astrologers had told young Thein Tin that the man she married would attain world renown. After the death of her father her mother had a dream which emphasized the prediction. Daw Kye said she saw a great spectacle of the sun, the revered peacock emblem, and the picture of her young daughter rising in the eastern skies. She called to Thein Tin's father to come and see the great sight, but when he arrived the daughter's likeness had disappeared. The mother was sure this meant that Thein Tin's father would never know the greatness into which their daughter would marry.

It seemed highly improbable in remote Pantanaw in 1934 that the name of Daw Thein Tin's husband would become a household word. But the Burmese have faith in their astrologers and dreams, and in this case it was justified.

Thein Tin was born and reared near the city of Mandalay, the former royal capital of Burma, and widely celebrated in a Kipling ballad. She was the only child of wealthy lawyer U Khinn. As she grew up, the girl showed qualities that Burmese like to find in their wives. She was wealthy and without dependents such as younger sisters and brothers; she had meekness, good looks and piety, and she was conscientiously applying herself to education. A future brother-in-law was to say that her greatest attribute was modesty, a natural legacy of her culture. Thein Tin was a teen-ager when her father died and she went with her mother to live with her maternal grandparents in Thant's home town. There she was graduated from high school. She never studied English because her conservative Buddhist parents said this was the language of heretics. She decided to continue her education by studying Pali, the language of the Buddhist scriptures, and was so deeply religious that there were reports she might even become a nun. However a distant cousin changed that. (Maung Thant's uncle had married the girl's aunt.)

Thant was born on January 22, 1909, to U Po Hnit and Daw Nan Thaung, who lived in one of the best houses in Pantanaw— a two-story teakwood structure on stilts which was the usual insurance against snakes and floods. They also owned several other houses, rice fields and garden land and a small herd of livestock —bullocks, buffaloes, and cows. Thant's grandparents had built up a modest fortune from the successful operation of a rice mill and the export of cottage-industry goods. His father was carrying on the family business in partnership with a rich uncle.

A week after the little boy was born, a naming ceremony was in order since he did not have even a family designation. His hair was washed for the first time. A relative, noticing the result, said the baby should be called Thant, which meant clean. His parents readily agreed—because they had selected that name for him too.

Thant was to acquire three younger brothers. They all had to observe certain household customs. For example, before going to bed each had to prostrate himself before the Lord Buddha's shrine and his parents. Thant's father was the only man in town who could read and write English—he had been to Calcutta to study. He also owned a library, where the future Secretary-General of the United Nations developed a voracious reading habit. One of Thant's first sorties into English was in an anthology that contained the story of the little Dutch boy who held his finger in the dike—a tale he had reason to remember years later when trying to hold back floods of world conflict.

Thant was fourteen when his father died and he became the head of a grief-stricken family. His mother soon found herself in straitened circumstances as a result of the handling of the estate by a relative whose operations were open to question. As a consequence, Thant decided that he could neither follow his chosen career of journalism nor complete four years at the university. Instead, he felt he should go to Rangoon for two years and then return home to earn enough money to enable his brothers to receive a higher education. At seventeen he went to the capital where he became active in the university's literary and debating circles, bombarded the press with letters and articles, and developed a friendship with U Nu, who later became Prime Minister.

In 1928 Maung Thant returned to Pantanaw and began teaching in the high school. He also successfully entered literary competitions, receiving one prize for his translation of *The Pied Piper of Hamelin* into Burmese. He won first place in the nation-wide Teachership Examination in 1931 and was named headmaster of the Pantanaw high school. When the position of superintendent of schools opened up, Thant suggested that Nu apply. He did and got the job. However, a little later the superintendent found it the better part of discretion to return to Rangoon after eloping with the daughter of the president of the school board. Thant was advanced to the vacancy.

It was Pantanaw's best-known educator and journalist who caught the attention of the studiously religious Thein Tin. There were other marks in his favor. He came from a conservative Buddhist family and had mastered the art of meditation which he practiced regularly. On Thant's side, however, there was a typically Burmese obstacle to the marriage. Thein Tin was older than he. His mother had just been through a similar crisis with Thant's brother Khant who had fallen in love with a girl his senior. The eldest son had sided with his mother in opposing the match, but Khant eloped to live happily and father five children. When Thant found himself interested in an older woman, elopement did not seem to be appropriate for the superintendent of schools. So the future diplomat undertook painstaking negotiations with his parent, which resulted in a conditional agreement. They could be married when Thant's second brother Thaung was graduated from Rangoon University and had entered government service.

The courtship between Thein Tin and Thant was scarcely in the Western fashion, which was not unexpected because of the nature of the parties and their tradition. Thant's friend Dr. Maung Maung is quoted as saying, "When Nu fell in love, he wrote poetry aflame with emotions and dedicated them, one and all, to the dear lady. When Thant fell in love he wrote letters to the editor, and articles, and a new book." * (The latter was a translation of the glories of ancient Athens and Rome for high school students.) As for the display of emotions which Westerners associate with romance, Thant expressed his views on that subject in a speech in Madison, Wisconsin, in July 1961. He said, "I was rather shocked by the public embracing in city parks . . . the American habit of using a parked car as a bedroom. Such behavior would be inconceivable in Burma."

The first child born to Daw Thein Tin and U Thant in 1936 was a bright, healthy boy. Suddenly, however, the child became ill. A monk was called in, who could do nothing about little Boh's racking cough. The worried father wrote to his brother on April 22, 1936: "People say that Maung Boh will be better after the customary naming ceremony. So it was performed yesterday . . . and about four hundred people were invited." The baby did improve, but within a few months he was fataly ill. On September 22, 1936, U Thant wrote U Khant: "Maung Boh died at 3:30 yesterday after a somewhat long illness. The loss shocks

* June Bingham, *U Thant*. Alfred A. Knopf, Inc., New York, 1966, p. 121.

us immensely. The loss is all the more keen as he was [an] exceptionally clever child. He had been ailing for the last ten days, but we had never thought that he would be cut off from us so soon. The burial took place on the same evening at 5 P.M. Ma Thein Tin is so much afflicted that her health is a matter of anxiety. I also feel like a man in a dream—and of course life is a long, long dream."

Friends brought the bereaved couple a four-month-old boy whose parents were giving him up in the hope that the infant would console them. They fell in love with the baby. Then their daughter Aye Aye was born, and finally their son Maung Tin Maung.

While Ma Thein Tin was absorbed with the cares of her family, her husband was following grave developments in the outside world—through shortwave radio and what newspapers and magazines were available to him. The Germans had driven into Poland and finally into the Low Countries and France. The Japanese had attacked Pearl Harbor. Then 1942 was upon them, and the Japanese were bombing and invading Burma. Refugees were clogging the roads in search of safety. The British blew up installations in Rangoon and retreated up the peninsula. By May, the country was in Japanese hands. Thant was called to Rangoon to draft recommendations for the improvement of Burmese education. With an anxious heart he left his family and made his way to the capital where he dodged bombs and worried about his home.

Thant's report was submitted, and that was the end of it. Daw Thein Tin's husband returned to Pantanaw in July, much to her relief. She did not then know that he joined a little group to listen to clandestine overseas broadcasts for he wanted to spare her the strain of guarding her talk in the presence of the Japanese. He maintained an outwardly correct behavior toward the invaders, removing books from his library that would give them any hint that he was anti-Fascist. Thant received his first assignment from the resistance movement when he was asked to help provide rice for a secret cache for the hour of a national uprising. He came under suspicion of the occupation officials when he failed to carry out their instructions to make Japanese the compulsory language in the schools. He staved off retribution by explaining that he could not find suitable teachers, but there was a warning that he was in danger of assassination.

Eventually, the resistance forces and the Allies were able to go on the offensive. They drove the Japanese out of Rangoon in May 1945. Then there began an effort to rebuild a shattered nation and give it a new political structure. This time it was to be one of independence from Britain. The schoolteacher from Pantanaw would be involved and gain a springboard to the fame the astrologers had predicted to Thein Tin. But this was not without a further searching of the stars.

After the war, Daw Thein Tin's husband became a vigorous exponent of democracy. He explained that "it substitutes reason and persuasion for force . . . and it makes possible a change of government without a violent upheaval. . . . Democracy is the keynote of the arch of human freedom. . . . What are its other stones?" he asked. These were his answers: "The first is personal freedom . . . the second is reign of law . . . the third . . . is freedom of thought, of worship, of speech, and of publication."

To carry out his ideas, Thant felt he must start a magazine like the *Atlantic Monthly*, with which he had long been familiar, to deal with the social, political, and economic issues confronting the Burmese people as they began to run their own affairs. To launch this project he felt it was necessary to move to Rangoon. The idea raised a storm of protest from his mother, the members of the school board, faculty, and students. They all wanted him to remain in Pantanaw and continue his educational activities while satisfying his journalistic urge on the side.

Only Daw Thein Tin favored the move to Rangoon. She remembered what the astrologers had said, and Pantanaw did not seem to be a likely locale for fulfillment of such a prophesy.

During the controversy over whether they should go to Rangoon, Thant came down with a mysterious illness. The astrologers were summoned. His mother described the situation this way, as recalled later by his brother Khant: "The abbot of Sein Monastery in Pantanaw ... examined U Thant's horoscope and predicted immense success in life if he moved to Rangoon and sought pastures anew there. He instructed [that] certain rites ... be performed to ward off evils. The rites ... were that one night U Thant should sleep with three bags of rice, one placed near his head, another about his middle, and the remaining near his feet. The next morning the rice put near his head should be cooked and offered to the Lord Buddha; the rice put near his middle distributed to beggars, and the rice put near his feet should be given away to the birds."

Unknown to Thant, his wife and mother carried out the prescribed ritual while he slept. He recovered, and in July 1947 the family moved to Rangoon with some of their possessions, leaving the library and files behind in Pantanaw. In the war-ravaged capital they found a livable house on a small piece of land with several smaller buildings which, as was expected, were soon occupied by relatives who helped with the housekeeping, gardening, and baby-sitting. But Daw Thein Tin's husband was not to start his magazine.

The political situation in Rangoon was hectic. Rival prewar leaders were attempting to win and maintain power with the support of hoodlum military groups armed with weapons scattered over the country. Maj. Gen. Aung San, who headed the Burma National Army during the Japanese occupation, had become premier and leader of an all-party front delegation which visited London in January 1947. They won British agreement for independence the following January. His party was given a resounding victory at the polls in April.

On Saturday morning, July 19, 1947, the governing Council presided over by Aung San, was working on plans for reconstruction of the nation and its independence, less than six months away. Suddenly four young men in uniform ran into the room and fatally shot the Burmese leader and six of his cabinet. One was missing—U Nu, president of the Assembly. The assassins raced to his office, only to find it empty. U Nu was at home because he had been forewarned by his astrologer that it would be very dangerous for him to go out that day. The mastermind behind the plot was prewar Prime Minister U Saw, who opposed Aung San's leadership. He was later tried and hanged.

On the afternoon of the multiple assassinations the British Governor called in U Nu and asked him to form a new Governing Council. Before the week was over, Nu summoned his friend U Thant and named him to serve as press officer in the preparation of Burma for its independence. Thant laid aside his personal journalistic plans to serve his country.

After Burma's independence, Thant became, in succession, Deputy to the Secretary of the Information Ministry, Director of Broadcasting, Secretary of Information and Chairman of the Film Board.

The new government faced many difficulties. One was the uprising of the Karens, who wanted a separate state. When they advanced on Pantanaw, Thant moved his mother to Rangoon. The rebels burned his family's houses as well as the home he and Daw Thein Tin owned. Nu sent Thant to the Karen Headquarters to try to arrange a cease-fire. The emissary was well received, but his mission was not successful. It was only in 1964 that settlement was reached with the insurgents; by that time, Daw Thein Tin's husband had become deeply involved in world crises. The Prime Minister assigned him one responsibility after another until Thant was Nu's chief consultant on foreign affairs, whether in Rangoon or during state visits to other countries.

As her husband's professional duties expanded, Daw Thein Tin was left increasingly with the upbringing of the children. Their foster son, Saw Lwin, became a truant from school and began secretly seeing a young girl. When the deception was uncovered, the foster father, ordinarily slow to anger, showed emphatic disapproval. The boy reacted by leaving home and eloping. He was publicly disowned by Thant. But Daw Thein Tin's motherly heart has always been touched by children, whether wayward or not. She maintained secret contact with Saw Lwin and his wife and contrived to send them money, which Thant learned about only years later.

In 1955, Daw Thein Tin became the mistress of a comfortable new yellow stucco house her husband had built for her on Windermere Road in Rangoon. However, Thant "lived in a suitcase," as one of his associates put it, traveling on diplomatic missions to many capitals, including Moscow and Peking. In 1957 Prime Minister Nu offered him the post of Permanent Representative of Burma to the United Nations. The man who had always wanted to be an educator and a journalist was pleased with the idea. At last he would be able to spend more time with his family. However, Daw Thein Tin was disturbed at the thought of such a radical change because of her health. She required specialized medical attention for high blood pressure. Her husband and U Nu both suggested that this might be more readily available in the United States. She yielded to the masculine persuasion. The yellow stucco house was rented, and the family of four boarded the plane for New York. It was a miserable trip for Daw Thein Tin, who suffered from airsickness.

On August 14, 1957, the Burmese Ambassador presented his credentials to Secretary-General Hammarskjöld. Daw Thein Tin could read what kind of a day it was from the now publicized page of her husband's diary, which he has kept conscientiously for more than a quarter of a century. The small, even script recounted:

> Office at 9:30 and went over the documents on the G.A. [General Assembly]
> Discussed Residential accommodation with Jimmy. So difficult to find a suitable apartment of about ten rooms (furnished) within the sanctioned rent of $1000 a month. Dictated a few correspondence and went to U.N. at 10:45 to present my credentials. Mr. Hammarskjold received me very warmly and recounted our meeting in July 1955 when he entertained U Nu, James * and me to a small lunch. He has a high esteem for U Nu for his moral and spiritual qualities. His knowledge of Buddhist philosophy, though not profound, is far from superficial. I am impressed by his interest in the moral and spiritual aspects of life. He makes some references to the affinity of approach between an Austrian philosopher † and Lord Buddha. I attempted to straighten him out on the theory of Kharma. A very pleasant and rewarding thirty minutes.
> Weather reminded me of Burma in April—hot and humid.
> Read Max Lerner's *America as a Civilization*—pp. 123-266.

* James Barrington, who preceded and followed Thant as Permanent Representative of Burma to the UN.
† Martin Buber.

Dag Hammarskjöld remarked to an aide one day that U Thant would make a good Secretary-General. The words were prophetic.

Although Thant was soon engrossed in his new responsibilities, the search for suitable living quarters for his family went on. At first they stayed at the Adams Hotel on East Eighty-sixth Street, then moved to an apartment on East Seventy-fourth Street which was demolished two years later; and finally ended up with a duplex on East Seventy-second. Here they learned that there can be something less than diplomacy in New York real-estate operations. They had sublet an eleven-room furnished apartment for $1,050 a month—the legal unfurnished rate was $402.50. In two years the tenant from whom they were leasing asked for $1,200 a month. A year after that, the Thants were told they must pay $7,000 for damages to the furnishings by their cat—whose claws had been drawn. The Acting Secretary-General volunteered still another increase, but he was now game for the headline hunters. In addition to stories about the pet, which Thant said sounded like a Bengal tiger, there appeared in print, tales about guests sleeping on the floors and throwing food out of the windows. The housing authorities reviewed the case. The court decided the sublet charge was outrageous and ordered a refund. Public opinion declined to take seriously the reports of riotous living in the Buddhist household, where the wife and mother was a semi-invalid. In August 1962 U Thant quietly moved his family to a secluded red-brick house in Riverdale on the Hudson River, which they rented from Lewis W. Douglas, former Ambassador to Great Britain. Here Daw Thein Tin found the isolation which her shy nature and fragile health required, since hope of returning soon to Burma had been buried under the weight of world responsibility that had suddenly shifted to her husband's shoulders.

The crash of a plane near Ndola, Northern Rhodesia, on September 17, 1961, was the final event in fulfilling the prophecy of the astrologers to the girl Thein Tin many years before. Secretary-General Hammarskjöld died in that accident. Grieving delegates turned from their sad tributes to the monumental task of electing his successor. The choice was difficult. The man would have to be approved by major factions in the cold war, and the Soviet Union had launched a campaign, even before the death of Hammarskjöld, to try to curb the power of the top UN post. After nearly two months of intensive consultation it was decided that the delegate from Burma should be named Acting Secretary-General for one year. On November 3, 1961, Daw Thein Tin sat in the crowded Assembly hall with her son, daughter, and son-in-law, Tin Myint U, and watched her husband take the oath of office. Before the Assembly voted on November 30, 1962, that U Thant should be Secretary-General in his own right for four years, the family circle had been broken. Maung Tin Maung was dead.

On May 21, 1962, the news tickers at the United Nations carried the shattering word that "Timmy," then a student at Hunter College, had fallen from a moving bus in Rangoon where he had gone to enroll at his father's old university. He was planning to return to New York for the summer. He had died of the brain injuries he sustained.

Aides carried the news of the tragedy to the father in the privacy of his office on the thirty-eighth floor of the United Nations. The tears came, but his first word was of Daw Thein Tin. He asked himself, "How can I tell my wife?"

The Secretary-General left his office and went to his home, where the family was alone with its grief for two days. The shock on top of Daw Thein Tin's ill health made it impossible for them to travel to Burma. And the world's responsibilities weighed on the father. On the day of the funeral, U Thant kept a speaking engagement at Carleton University in Ottawa. He had been offered a release, but he said, "The people have been so kind." His appeal at Carleton for the young to try "to save succeeding generations from the scourge of war" seemed to many like a personal memorial to Maung Tin Maung.

The frail mother became even more withdrawn as a result of the shock and grief, spending additional time in prayer and meditation. Aye Aye and her husband, now a teacher of mathematics at Manhattan College, moved into the Riverdale house to try to dispel some of the atmosphere of mourning. Saw Lwin was forgiven and brought to New York with his young family to live with his foster parents—once more to comfort them for the loss of a son.

On January 31, 1966, Aye Aye presented her parents with their first grandchild—a boy who was named Thant Myint U. The grandmother glowed over the bright horoscope of the infant with its promise of high position and fame.

Daw Thein Tin has always tried to create for her husband a home where he can find relaxation and escape from the burdens he carries through the day. At Bella Vista in Riverdale she has set up a kind of little Burma where he can cast off the cares of the world's most "impossible job," as a predecessor described it. She always wears the native *longyi* and usually, as Burmese tradition dictates, family diamonds. Her domain is essentially Western in this fifteen-room house with servants' quarters, tennis court, and swimming pool, where her husband finds his favorite recreation. The staff includes a cook, a maid, and a nurse for the baby. But the atmosphere evokes a Burma that is fondly remembered.

All her life Daw Thein Tin's religion has been a deep preoccupation for her. In her husband's study, which opens into a solarium lined with books and the autographed pictures of world statesmen, there is a small shrine with a sanctified statue of the Lord Buddha. No one steps on the holy rug lying before it without removing his shoes and Daw Thein Tin keeps fresh flowers, goblets of water, and offerings of rice on the altar.

Daw Thein Tin rarely attends a UN function. And only occasionally is there a luncheon or dinner at the Riverdale house to which non-Burmese are invited. U Thant has changed his routine from the days when as the delegate of Burma he felt free to entertain guests at New York restaurants. His high office requires a constant round of entertaining at the UN, often on a greater and more elaborate scale: luncheons in his suite on the thirty-eighth floor or in the Security Council Lounge, state dinners in the North Delegates Lounge. When he leaves the UN it is to go home, unless there is a function where his presence is a diplomatic must.

Thant's day begins at 6:30, when he arises and strives first to attain what he calls "emotional equilibrium" through the Buddhist rite of meditation. He says, however, that through years of disciplined practice, "I can meditate or pray anywhere—in my office, in my study at home, sitting in a plane. In Buddhism there is the supreme plane of Nirvana which we strive to attain, when man's mind and soul are completely free of all worldly thoughts. It is a very difficult stage to reach."

After his morning meditation, Thant reads the papers, frequently watches the *Today* television program, and eats a Western-style breakfast of bacon and eggs. A UN aide drives him to the office around nine o'clock. When he returns home in the evening it is anywhere from eight to nine o'clock. He puts on his *longyi* and reads the papers and then dines with Daw Thein Tin, and possibly other members of the family and friends, on his favorite Burmese food. Afterward if he has not taken copious files home for perusal he may read or watch a television program like *Danny Kaye* or boxing. Unless there is an emergency, he tries to keep Saturday to a half-day work schedule and Sunday completely free from official engagements.

Daw Thein Tin's greatest contribution to her husband's serenity may be her lack of personal involvement in his highly charged everyday world. She has been steeped in the tradition that Burmese women, although consulted by their husbands on important decisions, do not intrude into the masculine area of activity because of their recognition of the "nobility of manhood." An Asian woman has explained, "We call it *hpon,* the glory, the holiness of a man, and we respect this not with subservience but with the same feelings as we respect monks and parents. A wife does not throw her longyi across her husband's bed, she does not touch any of his possessions with her feet in carelessness, she uses a separate mug for her bathwater. A bad wife who does not respect her husband's manhood does him the greatest harm. . . ." *

In this tradition, Daw Thein Tin was consulted by her husband about whether he should make himself available for a new term as Secretary-General beginning on Nov. 3, 1966. She knew ahead of time what he would say in a letter to members of the Security Council on September 1. Thant wrote: "I have decided not to offer myself for a second term as Secretary-General."

U Thant explained to the delegates that a "variety of considerations—personal, official and political," had influenced his decision. Among the personal was a wish of Daw Thein Tin to return to Burma. However, as in the past, a devoted wife was ready to surrender her own inclination to the interest of her husband. A unanimous United Nations urged U Thant to

* Mi Mi Khaing, *Burmese Family*. Indiana University Press, Bloomington, Indiana, 1962, p. 71.

change his mind. His wife agreed in advance to his reply when he went before the General Assembly on December 2, 1966 to say, "I accept today a fresh five-year-term as Secretary-General of the United Nations in response to the wishes of the Security Council and the General Assembly."

Imelda Romualdez Marcos with her husband,
Ferdinand Marcos

10.

Imelda Romualdez Marcos—Republic of the Philippines

N an early spring night in 1954 Imelda Romualdez, a recent beauty queen, was lounging comfortably on the patio of the Manila home of a cousin when the telephone rang. It was her host, Daniel Romualdez, bank president, chairman of the Rehabilitation Corporation, dean of a law college, and member of Congress. He was about to take over the gavel as Speaker pro tempore for debate on the national budget. He predicted there would be verbal fireworks when the brilliant minority critic—Ferdinand E. Marcos—took the floor and suggested that his wife bring Meldy, as their guest was known to family and friends, to watch the fun. Without bothering to change, put on makeup, or comb their hair, the two women jumped into the car and were soon standing in the doorway of the House of Representatives. They were so casually attired they decided not to go to the visitors' gallery. As Marcos arose to attack the extravagance of the Magsaysay administration, Mrs. Romualdez whispered to Meldy, "Listen to him, he's really good."

Meldy chewed watermelon seeds she had bought from a street vendor and noted the handsome man who had begun to speak. As a singer, she was immediately impressed by the rich baritone voice and the speaker's eloquence as he changed with ease and perfect diction from English to Spanish to Tagalog. However, Marcos had two drawbacks in Meldy's view: he was short and he was a member of the Liberal Party.

As the hour grew late, Romualdez sent word for the women to wait for him in the air-conditioned cafeteria. They had just followed instructions when the door opened and Ferdinand Marcos walked in. He saw the beautiful Meldy, whose windblown hair emphasized her loveliness. He stopped and stared, expecting an introduction at once. Many of the onlookers knew of his reputation for romantic exploits and were hesitant to take any responsibility for opening the way to yet another. Finally, an old political friend agreed to do the honors. Never one to stand on ceremony when he had a goal in view, Marcos immediately asked the somewhat startled Meldy to stand up. When she did so, he placed himself back to back with her and verified the fact that he was half an inch taller. (She was wearing flat heels!)

"Fine," said Marcos with finality to the Congressman who had presented him, "everything is OK. I'm getting married."

The Romualdezes were well aware of Marcos' self-confidence as a Lothario, so they quickly whisked Meldy out of the cafeteria and away from the presence of the brash young man, taking her back to the shelter of their home.

Imelda was accustomed to receiving attention from admirers,

frequently in the form of large bouquets of roses. The next day as she sat at her desk in the Central Bank she was not impressed by the delivery of two roses, one a bud and one full-blown. Attached was a card which read, "Everything is so rosy. I wonder why? Ferdinand." A colleague explained that according to the custom in the north of the country this was a marriage proposal—the blooming rose symbolized the giver's love while the bud carried his hope that the recipient would respond in kind. Imelda was intrigued but annoyed by what she considered a typical display of Marcos' stampede strategy. She who had beauty, wealth, and talent, and belonged to the most important political family in Leyte was not about to be swept off her feet by a boor—particularly when he was only half an inch taller, thirteen years older, and a Liberal to boot. She promptly declined his invitation to lunch.

That same night Speaker Romualdez made another telephone call to his home just as Meldy and his wife were returning in high-fashion evening clothes from a recital. This time it was a plea for help. Marcos had started a filibuster against the budget. The Speaker pro tempore asked that they come back to the House because it was hoped that when Ferdinand saw Meldy in her glamorous finery, he would be lured from the floor. Then the other lawmakers could get the budget approved. Meldy agreed to play the beautiful decoy. As it turned out, she was not needed to save the Philippine budget, but her appearance was a step on the road toward the most important decision in her life.

Marcos had already concluded that he had done all he could to obstruct the money legislation when Meldy walked into the visitors' gallery. He promptly joined her and did not even bother to answer the roll call on the final vote. However, the fair lady was not to be won easily. She rebuffed his suggestion that they dine the next night. Marcos' next tack was to try to find out where Meldy planned to spend the approaching Easter holiday. Ferdinand knew that Romualdez and his wife were going to Hong Kong, so he assumed the beauteous cousin would accompany them. He booked a seat on the same plane. When he arrived at the airport he discovered that Mr. and Mrs. Romualdez were alone. Promptly dropping the idea of the Hong Kong trip, he rushed to the Romualdez home. There he found a cluster of children about to take off for Baguio in Luzon, with Meldy as their baby-sitter. There was a shortage of transportation for the five-hour trip, so Ferdinand offered to drive his scornful love. She consented—but wedged two youngsters between herself and the driver.

By this time, the romance being pursued with such vigor by the outstanding war hero, trial lawyer, and eminent bachelor was the talk of the Philippines. However, the subject of Ferdinand Marcos' intentions seemed immovable. Imelda had a deep sense of religious obligation instilled in her by the Spanish tradition in her family, so his aggressive suit during Holy Week annoyed her. When he waylaid her on the way to church, she was angry. When she finally admitted him to the house, it was to ignore him. So he made friends with the youngsters and induced them to press his case. Meldy's interest was suddenly aroused when she saw the way he could entertain children. Here was humility and imagination she had never suspected.

The people of Baguio began to cast horoscopes about the man who, it was said in the north, was destined to be President, and the young woman who looked and acted like a President's wife. The two readings were found to be conjunctive. Ferdinand was so elated that he tried to kiss Meldy. He failed, but she did invite him to mass the next day. There she discovered he was not only devout but knew the mass by heart. They had their first date that afternoon—at a tea dance in the Country Club. Three days later Ferdinand invited Meldy to breakfast—it was the Saturday before Easter and he had also assembled some cousins. He then confronted his love in the presence of witnesses with all the necessary papers for a civil marriage. She offered various excuses to try to stave off the coup—it was Holy Week, her father did not know, and the like. However, the undaunted suitor was prepared to overcome all resistance. Just eleven days after they had met they were married by a justice of the peace in the little town of La Trinidad, close to the Benguet gold mine where the bridegroom had once worked. Marcos gave his bride a ring with eleven diamonds. Two weeks later Meldy's family had a splendid wedding for their daughter in the Manila Procathedral with President Magsaysay as the principal sponsor of the bride. He also hosted an elaborate wedding breakfast for three thousand guests on the grounds of the Presidential Palace.

The bridal couple left on a honeymoon to Hong Kong, Ottawa, where Marcos was an observer at the Colombo Conference of Asian Nations involving reciprocal trade; and then New York for the groom to head the Philippine Delegation to the United Nations General Assembly. Ferdinand and Imelda, in fact, were beginning a journey that was to take them to the Presidential Palace in Manila in a dozen years.

Imelda Romualdez was born in 1931, the oldest of her father's second group of children. Her Roman Catholic family, largely of the Nationalist Party, was the most powerful politically in Leyte and Samar. Her father, Vincente, was dean of St. Paul's Law College. Meldy took her Bachelor of Science degree at the College, receiving a teacher's certificate. Her comeliness, however, attracted more attention than her academic accomplishments. At eighteen she was selected as the Rose of Tacloban, Leyte, for the city flower festival. The reasons were obvious. Her measurements were 36-23-35, and a family admirer, Hartzell Spence, later described the beauty queen this way:

"Meldy was a big, long-limbed girl. When she piled her sleek jet hair on her head in a Burmese bun, she was classic Malayan, with large black sloe eyes, broad intellectual forehead, high but not prominent cheekbones in a heart-shaped face, a softly rounded chin, fine neck and shoulders, thin waist; the prototype of what every Malay-descended girl would like to be. Because of the Spanish admixture, she was tall for an Asian, just over five feet six inches, and with her hair set high she overcast most of her acquaintances—and all of her boy friends." *

Her beauty and her voice—one singing teacher predicted that with adequate training she could become the nation's Renata Tebaldi—combined to win her a place of honor at the Philippines International Fair and Exposition. She went on to be named Miss Philippines in 1954, the year she met Ferdinand Marcos. However, Meldy's beauty-contest career came to an abrupt end when she was asked to represent her country in the Miss Universe Contest. Vincente Romualdez set his foot down sternly on the prospect of a possible motion-picture contract. Beauty contests in the Philippines are often won by young women of social prestige as well as beauty, who thereby attain a kind of "deb of the year" status. Father Romualdez adamantly refused to have his daughter associated with any commercialization of this ritual.

After college, Meldy went to Manila to live with her cousin and his wife and took a job at the Central Bank on the staff of the house organ. After office hours she studied singing. Her teacher suggested that she enroll at the Philippine Women's

* Hartzell Spence, *For Every Tear a Victory: The Story of Ferdinand E. Marcos.* McGraw-Hill Book Co., Inc., New York, 1964.

University for formal vocal training. She continued her singing lessons until her children began to arrive following her marriage to the "Golden Voice from the North." She also used her vocal talent to promote Ferdinand's successful political career. The duets of Meldy and Ferdinand Marcos, while stumping nearly every barrio in the islands during the 1965 Presidential election campaign, added grace notes to the longest, costliest and most acrimonious contest in Philippine history. One observer estimated that the beautiful, handsomely dressed, sweet-voiced Meldy was worth a million votes to her husband.

The man whose romantic blitz captured Imelda Romualdez had long been a controversial figure. He was born in Sarrat, in Ilocos Norte province on Luzon, on Sept. 11, 1917, the elder of two sons whose teacher-lawyer-politician father, Mariano, was a severe disciplinarian. Ferdinand, a brilliant law student at the University of the Philippines, became national small-bore rifle champion and a member of the boxing, swimming and wrestling teams. When he went home on holiday in September 1935, the first election was being held under the new commonwealth status granted by the United States. Ferdinand's father was a candidate for Congress in an angry campaign. Three days after Mariano Marcos was defeated by Julio Nalundasan, the victor was shot through the heart with a .22-caliber rifle. There was gossip immediately, but it was not until Ferdinand was a senior in law school, four years later, that he was accused of the crime. A trial in which he was convicted became a national political issue. He refused a Presidential pardon. While out of prison on bail he achieved the highest grade in the Philippine bar examination. He then argued his own appeal before the Supreme Court—and was acquitted.

Meldy, like all Filipinos, was well acquainted with this colorful chapter in the life of the suitor who so ardently pursued her in 1954. She also knew about his outstanding war record—wounded five times as a guerrilla officer when the Japanese invaded the islands in 1941, a captive of the Japanese who tortured him, commended by Gen. Douglas MacArthur for his efforts to defend Bataan, and the recipient of twenty-two American and Philippine medals. When Meldy married Ferdinand, he was a Liberal member of Congress for five years. With her at his side he went on to the Senate five years later by the greatest plurality in a Philippine election and became president of that body in 1963. They have three children. Imelda, nicknamed Imee, was born prematurely in 1955—her mother had been modeling maternity clothes at a charity fashion show; Ferdinand, Jr., affectionately known as Bong-bong, appeared in 1958, while Irene or Rena arrived in 1960.

It was the 1965 Presidential campaign that proved how valuable Imelda was as a political partner of the ambitious man she had married. Although one of her first objections to Ferdinand had been that he belonged to the Liberal Party, while she was from a family of Nacionalistas, that deficiency was remedied in 1964. Diosdado Macapagal decided that he wanted to run for a second term, although the Filipinos had never elected a President to two full terms. Marcos also had an eye on the job, so he bolted to the Nationalist Party and soon was the leading challenger of the President.

The fight was on, and Meldy, always at her husband's side was to say after the victory, "I believe that I can safely say that I am the most traveled President's wife. . . . I have been to nearly every town in the Philippines. I have firsthand knowledge of the situation in every part." The Marcos traveled in an air-conditioned Ford Galaxy except where the rough going required a jeep. They averaged twenty handshakes a minute, wore leis of the national flower, sampaguita, and sang duets. The effusive

Ferdinand promised the voters, "I will give you everything you want—except my wife." Meldy kept up a pace that would have taxed the stamina of a prizefighter at the height of his condition, sometimes wearing the hot but popular native *terno* with its butterfly sleeves, changing as often as eight times a day —frequently in the car—swallowing ever-present mosquitoes as she sang with her husband in the villages, many nights existing on four hours' sleep, pressing on in spite of colds. Her greatest trial was separation from the children. She said, "The campaign was hard on the children." They had been sick often, sometimes hospitalized. Moreover, there was the reaction of the children to dark charges being made against their father in such a free-wheeling campaign. Ferdinand and Imelda had forbidden Imee, Bong-bong, and Rena to listen to radio or watch television to try to protect them from the accusations being hurled at the Nacionalista candidate. However, the youngsters could not be insulated from their contacts with other children. One day Ferdinand, Jr., came home with what was called the Liberal Party "hymnbook," and asked, "Mama, where is the land Daddy grabbed?" Meldy related later how she "told the children little by little about the accusations, that there was no such land, that their father was being maligned by his enemies." From that time on the vindication of the Marcos name became the primary objective of Imelda, with the winning of the Presidency by her husband only secondary. For she said she thought to herself, "Imagine if the children were to wake up one day to find their name forever smeared! This is what Ferdinand's victory means to me now: that the people have seen the truth with us." *

There was a charge against Meldy, too, in the campaign— that she had posed nude for cheap magazines and movies. This

* *New York Times*, November 28, 1965.

apparently arose from her brief beauty-contest career. According to Ron de Paolo in the Asian edition of *Life*, Imelda deftly parried charges against herself as well as those that her husband was a murderer, "as she now recalls, placing her well-manicured hands on her bosom, 'I would tell them in the barrios that I would not disgrace my family by posing for those movies, and that I could not be married—to that kind of man. If he was a beast, I would not be married to him and would be happier dead. Once they saw what kind of woman I was, they knew the truth.' " *

The election victory for Ferdinand and Meldy was a substantial one. The two candidates spent a total of eight million dollars in all, while eight million Filipino voters went to the polls, with a resulting margin for Marcos of more than 630,000. The Rose of Tacloban had become First Lady of the Philippines and the mistress of Malacañang, the rambling former summer palace built on the Pasig River in 1802. With the election over, the First-Lady-to-be told a reporter, "I am definitely off politics now. I will leave politics and government to my husband. Now I can go back to my role of wife and mother—and yes, caretaker of the home." This responsibility, of course, includes looking after her husband. "I have great faith in Ferdinand's talent and dedication," Meldy says. "I have to take good care of him more now that he is public property. Before I owed it to myself and the children to preserve his health. Now I owe it to the whole country."

As for the children, Meldy said after the election, "I sincerely want to keep them out of it as much as possible. This will pass —it's very temporary and they must grow up in a normal way."

Mrs. Marcos told a reporter for the *Philippines Free Press* in

* August 8, 1966 (reproduced in Presidential press kit for United States trip).

the spring of 1966 how she was trying to bring up the children of the President: "I have three well-adjusted children; all of them are at the top of their class. When I take them to Philippine Education they head for the books, not the toys. Every year I spend more than two thousand pesos on their books alone. At first they felt quite lonesome here in Malacañang. They had no neighbors. But now they invite friends over and they love riding on the Pasig. We have explained to them that, as children of the President of the Philippines, it is their duty to behave nicely. No, I don't think the palace will spoil them. In the first place, I don't think they have been in the public part of the palace more than four or five times since we moved here.

"I try to keep Bong-bong close to his father, so he will learn much. He went with his father to the opening of the Chamber of Agriculture and rode on a tractor. He went with his father to Fort Magsaysay and rode on a helicopter. He's learning judo now, and swimming, and horseback riding. The girls are learning Hawaiian dancing and ballet. I take them to fashion shows and polo games and parties. I have no trouble with them. My oldest girl—her school doesn't give medals and she felt so disappointed. So we bought medals and had our own ceremony and the President pinned six medals on her."

The palace into which Meldy moved her family was hardly a comfortable home in her view. It did not have a hot-water system; the central air-conditioning was not working, leaving the bedrooms stifling in the hot climate; the bathrooms needed repair; the water pipelines dated back to the time of the first American governors-general, and what linens remained were threadbare. The family's living quarters needed particular attention. Yielding to superstition, the Marcoses did not move into the palace wing which had been occupied by Presidents

Roxas and Magsaysay, both of whom died in office, or the rooms that were living quarters for Presidents Garcia and Macapagal, who had been defeated for reelection. Instead, a former reception room was converted into the master bedchamber, with separate rooms for the children. Glass-encased closets were crowded into an adjoining passageway for the family's clothes. They showed the President's attachment for elevator shoes, dark suits, and sports attire.

The style and flair for fashion displayed by the First Lady's extensive wardrobe led to comparisons with Mrs. Jacqueline Kennedy. Meldy resisted efforts to associate her with the former American First Lady, telling more than one interviewer, "I would rather be myself. I have no wish to be a fashion plate or set any trend in fashion." Leading Philippine designers compete for the patronage of Imelda Marcos because she is a striking showcase for their creations. Her clothes are mostly of Philippine origin, but there is an occasional Paris gown and an Italian knit, while some of her suits are acquired in New York and San Francisco. However, she is emphasizing the importance of buying in the Philippines. "I can get a wonderful wardrobe right here in Manila. . . . I use three couturiers here and shop at one particular store. . . ." Although she wears the native *terno* with flair when the public occasion demands, the one-time beauty queen prefers sheaths and slim two-piece dresses. Her color taste includes beige and pale sea shades of blue, green, and aqua, but she confesses, "I have worn chartreuse, shocking pink, and canary yellow when I wanted people to spot me in a room." When it seemed appropriate during her trying campaign travels she slipped into a *malong*—a wide tubular garment. She admits, "It is my favorite practical garment. Think of it, it can be used as a sarong, even for bathing. If it is cold, one can pull it up to the neck for warmth. If the sun is too hot on the head, it is just a matter of drawing it up over the hair and the whole garb is still flattering." She finds occasions when slacks are called for, as when she climbed the Lapu-lapu Mountain to bring relief to the victims of the Iloilo volcanic disaster. She also wears slacks when sailing, her favorite recreation.

In another respect there are those who find certain points of comparison between Mrs. Marcos and both Mrs. Kennedy and Mrs. Lyndon Johnson. This is because of her interest in beautification and the arts. At her first luncheon for reporters after taking up life in the Presidential palace, the First Lady expressed her desire to beautify the capital city. She declared, "I will try to beautify Manila—and yes, the rest of the country. I know that is rather an ambitious plan. But I will try to get the cooperation of the governors' wives. . . ." She wanted to provide incentives for local artists—to help musicians, writers, painters, and all those who were gifted. She recognized the need for a national building or auditorium where ballets, plays, concerts, and art exhibits could be held. But she also knew that her husband had come to power at a time when the Philippine treasury was almost bare and the economy was limping seriously. Under any circumstances the raising of 35 million pesos for a Philippine cultural center would be difficult. At first the task looked impossible, for Mrs. Marcos conceded, "We cannot talk of concerts and paintings if so many of our people cannot afford three square meals a day." Nevertheless, four months after the inauguration of her husband, invitations were issued from Malacañang Palace for ground-breaking ceremonies of the cultural center. Mrs. Marcos had obtained private financial pledges to go ahead with the project, secured an ideally located tract of land at the edge of Manila Bay for the location of the center, and had commissioned prize-winning architect Leandro V. Locsin to design the complex. It will have a theater for the performing arts, museum pavilions, a library, lecture halls, work-shops, an outdoor art gallery and an outdoor amphitheater. The center is also to serve as a repository of the nation's cultural heritage. The completion date is expected to be late 1968 or early 1969. In connection with her beautification program, the First Lady has also started a tree-planting campaign that she hopes will amount to the planting of some two million trees every year.

For her own activities Mrs. Marcos has set four goals. In addition to the cultural and beautification programs, she wants to attract more tourists to the Philippines. The elaborate press kit for reporters who covered the visit of President and Mrs. Marcos to the United States in September 1966 was liberally stuffed with tourist brochures. The First Lady's fourth goal is to promote the social welfare of the poor and underprivileged. These unfortunate ones came to her particular attention during the political campaigning with her husband. In this area, she says children should have top priority attention, followed by juvenile delinquents, unmarried mothers, prisoners, the sick, mentally retarded, and the aged.

The First Lady of the Philippines carries her responsibilities with the help of a press assistant, a woman who shops for gifts, one who manages the Heroes Hall in the Palace, gardeners, and a housekeeping staff. In addition, she is surrounded by a coterie of 150 volunteer associates known as the Blue Ladies. Imelda has explained the origin of this group to reporters: "I had several dozens of friends who were watching me campaign and who wanted to help me. More and more volunteers came. With my support and my help they banded together, all one hundred and fifty of them. They had spirit and energy. . . . These ladies have come down from their ivory towers and developed a social conscience. Many of them said they were miserable before they joined up. They were nervous and irritable, constantly worried over their husbands, who were too busy earning money. Now there are no more nervous tensions. Going out to the barrios has improved everyone's attitude, including mine. By going out to meet the barrio people I discovered the real cause of Ferdinand's crusade. . . . I will keep the Blue Ladies about me. They will be there to help in community improvement, they will become a civic group. . . .

"I will not have a kitchen cabinet. It came in for real criticism in the past when the public would observe some women sticking to the First Lady for social gains. My friends will not have to stick to anybody, even to a First Lady, to achieve social prominence. They were in Manila's Four Hundred even before they joined me."

With all of her preoccupations, Mrs. Marcos says she will never lose sight of her primary responsibility. "I am a wife first before a mother. I met my husband first and it is my first duty to see to it that our President's physical, mental and spiritual well-being are ensured."

This is Mrs. Marcos' formula: "The President and I see as much of each other as ever. We have our meals together. We are both very busy, but we try to work together, we inspire each other. Never say marriage is a fifty-fifty proposition. In marriage, I feel, you must give a hundred. I told the President: 'If you give me fifty, you will get a hundred and twenty in return.' I am essentially a happy person. Even when a schoolgirl, I was always happy. But my feet are on the ground even when people may be thinking I must be up in the clouds."

When President Marcos visited the United States in September 1966 to talk with President Johnson and address the United

Nations General Assembly, Meldy Marcos was at his side. Her beauty and charm were remarked upon wherever she went. However, the First Lady, as always, was concerned about the image of her husband. She confided after a Marcos television appearance that perhaps she should have advised Ferdinand beforehand how to answer some of the questions.